**DATE DUE**

Metro Litho
Oak Forest, IL 60452

|  |  |  |  |
|---|---|---|---|
|  |  |  |  |
|  |  |  |  |
|  |  |  |  |
|  |  |  |  |
|  |  |  |  |
|  |  |  |  |
|  |  |  |  |
|  |  |  |  |
|  |  |  |  |
|  |  |  |  |
|  |  |  |  |
|  |  |  |  |
|  |  |  |  |
|  |  |  |  |

*Hernando De Soto*

# THE WORLD'S GREAT EXPLORERS

## *Hernando De Soto*

By Robert Carson

Ⓟ CHILDRENS PRESS ®
CHICAGO

*De Soto and his men met with both
beauty and danger as they trudged
through the Florida swamps.*

Project Editor: Ann Heinrichs
Designer: Lindaanne Donohoe
Cover Art: Steven Gaston Dobson
Engraver: Liberty Photoengraving

**Library of Congress
Cataloging-in-Publication Data**
Carson, Robert, 1932-
    Hernando de Soto  / by Robert Carson.
       p.   cm. — (The World's great explorers)
    Includes bibliographical references and index.
    Summary: A biography of the Spanish explorer
who became the first European to reach the Missis-
sippi River.
    ISBN 0-516-03065-5
    1. Soto, Hernando de, ca. 1500–1542—Juvenile
literature. 2. Explorers—America—Biography—
Juvenile literature. 3. Explorers—Spain—Biogra-
phy—Juvenile literature. 4. America—Discovery and
exploration—Spanish—Juvenile literature. [1. De
Soto, Hernando, ca. 1500–1542. 2. Explorers.] I.
Title. II. Series.
E125.S7C37  1991              91–12665
970.01'6'092—dc20          CIP
[B]                          AC

*Hernando De Soto's arrival at the Mississippi River*

# Table of Contents

# Chapter 1
# The Father of the Waters

The column of Spanish soldiers slogged through the marshy, tangled forest, pushing toward higher ground that the Indians had told them lay ahead. They slashed vines and branches with their swords and battle-axes, slapped at mosquitoes, and were always wary of venomous snakes lurking in the foliage.

They were a gaunt, ragged band of men, some wearing crude sandals made of bark. A lucky few were still shod in patched leather boots that had been new when they landed on the Florida coast two years before. Since then, they had made an astonishing march of more than 1,500 miles (2,414 kilometers) through the wilderness of North America.

Some had started on horseback. But most of these bearded adventurers had walked every step, fighting off hostile Indians, swimming rivers, and wading through swamps like the one they found themselves in today. Most would have turned back long ago except for the iron will of the man who commanded them, Hernando De Soto, an imperial knight of Spain.

Today, as usual, De Soto himself walked at the head of the column, a tall, broad-shouldered figure of extraordinary strength. He was a superb horseman and swordsman. In fighting with the lance, he was said to be the best warrior in the Spanish empire.

Like the men who followed him, De Soto was weakened by the hardships and battles of the last two years. Yet today he pressed eagerly toward his goal, which was not the silver or gold most Spaniards were striving to gain. Now he was in quest of a river.

The Indians had told him it was the greatest stream on earth, so magnificent that they called it the Father of the Waters—in their language, the *Mississippi*.

The Spaniards broke free of the swamp, moving faster now on a long, gradual slope of thinly forested land. De Soto glimpsed a flash of water, the outline of a river, its surface gleaming in the spring sunshine.

At last they reached its bank, on the western edge of present-day Mississippi. There the Spaniards stood in awe, gazing across two miles (three kilometers) of rolling water toward the distant shore. This river was indeed worthy of its name; it was the king of all the streams of North America. None of them had ever seen, probably never imagined, a river of such breadth and majesty.

Hernando De Soto had already lived a life crowded with adventure. He was among the conquerors of the fabled Inca kingdom of Peru and had been a military captain in Panama, Honduras, and Nicaragua. But in centuries to come, he would be remembered for this day, May 8, 1541, when he reached the Mississippi River after his amazing journey across almost half a continent.

Perhaps he knew this was his greatest hour, for he dropped to his knees to give thanks for being allowed so great a feat. At that moment, the grandeur of the river may well have made his fierce struggle to reach it seem worthwhile.

*De Soto on the shore of the Mississippi River*

# Chapter 2
## The Heirs of Amadís

*"He will be the flower of the knights. . . . He will make strong men tremble, will accomplish things in which all others have failed."*
—*Amadís of Gaul, Book I*

**H**ernando De Soto was born into a world as fierce and restless as a nest of hawks. In 1500, the year De Soto is believed to have been born, Spain was a newly united nation, scarred by seven centuries of almost continual war. Most of that time, the Spaniards fought to drive out the Moors, people of the Muslim faith who invaded from North Africa. Before they were finally expelled, the Moors controlled most of Spain and Portugal. When not battling the Moors or joining crusades to the Holy Land, Spaniards often made war upon each other, region against region, one clan or family of nobles against another.

Soldiers became the honored men of the country. Eventually, becoming a soldier was almost the only way an ambitious youth could rise in the world. To be a warrior was glorious; other occupations seemed lowly and dull.

Nowhere in Spain was this feeling stronger than in the province of Extremadura. This impoverished corner of southwestern Spain produced not only De Soto but such adventurers as Hernando Cortés, conqueror of Mexico, and Francisco Coronado, who explored from Mexico all the way to what is now Kansas. Alvar Núñez Cabeza de Vaca, pathfinder in the American Southwest, was another son of Extremadura.

This province is a harsh land where brutal sun beats down on its few stunted trees and on fields yielding little more than clouds of dust. Extremadura had little to offer the world except the fierceness and daring of its sons. Since the Moorish wars had ended, the province, like all of Spain, bristled with unemployed warriors.

The love of valor and combat showed early in a boy's life. De Soto was born in a town called Jerez de los Caballeros, a name honoring an order of knights; its boys grew up playing rough games with wooden swords and lances. The most popular book of the time was called *The Virtuous Knight Amadís of Gaul.* Its hero, Amadís, falls in love with Oriana, an English princess. But he cannot marry her until he proves his courage in a dozen fantastic adventures in faraway places. Young Hernando, as soon as he learned to read, was deeply moved by these tales of chivalry and romance. All his life he would long to be another Amadís, to do amazing deeds in strange lands. Hernando was only one of countless Spanish youths who thought of themselves as heirs and followers of Amadís, the ideal knight.

Where could such adventures be found? In Spain, the answer was clear. Only a few years before De Soto's birth, Christopher Columbus had reached the

*Vasco Núñez de Balboa, one of Extremadura's famous explorers*

New World, and already Spain was rife with tales of fabulous wealth and glory to be gained there. Not only were there cities of gold, people said, but such marvels as a fountain of youth, races of giants, and tribes of Amazons.

A neighbor of the De Soto family, Vasco Núñez de Balboa, had already visited the Indies, as the newly found islands were called. By this time, people knew that these "Indies" were not in Asia, as Columbus had thought. Rather, they were part of another continent altogether. Everyone in town talked of Balboa's deeds and discoveries.

Hernando listened eagerly to tales of travelers returning from long voyages. The De Sotos were a family of minor nobility but little wealth. Such riches as the family possessed would one day go to Hernando's older brother. Hernando's mother hoped the boy would become a scholar or a priest. But even as a child, he excelled in mock duels with his playmates, both on foot and horseback. Hernando's mind was made up early: he would be an adventurer.

When he reached his early teens, Hernando was already taller and stronger than most grown men. At the same time, the De Soto family became short of money. Hernando had to find some way to support himself and, for a youth of nobility, common labor was out of the question, a disgrace.

Hernando's father sent the boy off to the port city of Seville with a letter of introduction to a nobleman named Pedro Arias Dávila. Usually known as Don Pedrarias, this man was one of King Ferdinand's most trusted military leaders.

Hernando rode from Extremadura on his horse, Lucerno, by far his most valuable possession. In Spain at the time, to have a horse was to be a gentleman; to travel on foot, as most people did, was common and undignified.

Young Hernando arrived in a city teeming with excitement and activity. A new expedition was being outfitted, a fleet to sail for distant Panama, then called Darién. The New World so gripped the imaginations of Spaniards that three thousand men had gathered in Seville, eager to sail. Many had sold farms, cattle, and houses to pay their way on a venture they felt sure would win them the gold and jewels of the Indies. They talked eagerly of pearls and of cannibal Indians

*A seventeenth-century map of Panama, then called Darién*

who shot poisoned arrows. All day long, wagons creaked through the streets hauling weapons, powder kegs, smoked hams, dried fruits, and all the other provisions to load twenty ships for the great voyage.

Hernando was granted an interview with Colonel Pedrarias, commander of the expedition and new governor of Panama. When he entered the colonel's room at the inn, he saw a fierce old warrior with a nose like the beak of an eagle. At age seventy, Pedrarias was still vigorous and strong and looked no more than middle-aged despite his white hair. He was known for enforcing harsh discipline, even amounting to cruelty. Here was a man to be feared and obeyed.

Pedrarias accepted Hernando as a page in his household. Young De Soto would make the voyage he had dreamed of to the New World. If he did well, eventually he would become a full-fledged knight with his own special horse and armor.

One of Hernando's first duties was to help prepare shipboard chambers for the governor's wife, the high-ranking noblewoman Isabel de Bobadilla, and her two daughters, Isabel and Elvira. As he worked arranging furnishings, he could not have imagined what important roles these women would later play in his life.

On April 11, 1514, young Hernando De Soto sailed from Spain, leaving behind his boyhood, voyaging toward adventures that would be among the most remarkable in history.

During the long weeks of the voyage, Hernando learned some hard lessons about this world he was

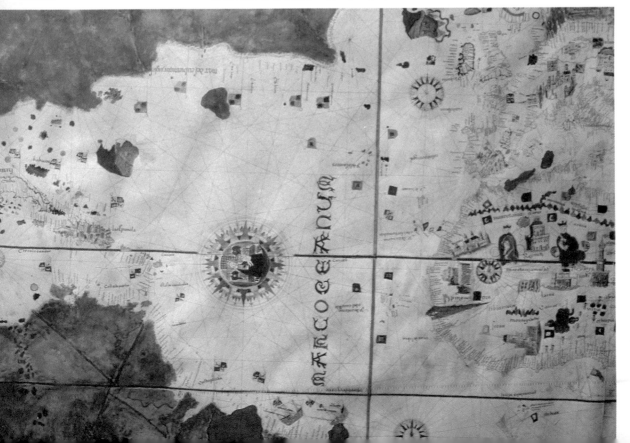

*Map drawn by Juan de la Cosa, mapmaker to Christopher Columbus, in about 1500. This was the first map to show the Caribbean Ocean.*

entering. In the twenty-two years since the first discoveries of Columbus, the Spaniards had quickly and ruthlessly expanded their empire in the Caribbean. The first people they enslaved and slaughtered were the Arawak Indians of an island Columbus named Hispaniola, today occupied by Haiti and the Dominican Republic. The greedy eyes of the conquerors next fell upon Puerto Rico and Jamaica. Soon after that came the turn of fertile Cuba.

Meanwhile, the great captain Vasco Núñez de Balboa, who was truly an explorer and not merely a bandit, had established a settlement on the isthmus of Panama, then called Darién. He had befriended the Indians and they led him to the vast Pacific Ocean. News of some of Balboa's achievements had reached Spain, but when De Soto sailed, the Pacific was still unknown to Europeans.

*Sixteenth-century map of the island of Hispaniola, which is occupied today by Haiti and the Dominican Republic*

*Balboa's famous entry aboard a ship to Darién, hidden inside a pork barrel*

Although Balboa's deeds were the talk of Spain, talk on the ship was jealous gossip about the explorer. He was too friendly with the Indians, his rivals said; they whispered that he was disloyal to the king. Balboa had even made his voyage from Cuba to Darién hidden inside a barrel of pork to escape his creditors. "Disgraceful!" said some of the officers on De Soto's ship, and they plotted his destruction.

Hernando quickly became friends with Diego San Martín, a young man older than Hernando who had worked for Governor Pedrarias for five years. From San Martín, Hernando heard a strange story about Pedrarias. The governor always kept a coffin under his bed, and once a year he slept in it, murmuring

*Spanish galleon*

prayers all through the night. This odd practice, Pedrarias believed, had kept him strong and enabled him to outlive his many enemies.

If Pedrarias was strange and savage, his wife, Dona Isabel, seemed just the opposite. One of the most-admired noble ladies of Spain, she won special permission to bring her two younger daughters on this voyage. Hernando often accompanied Dona Isabel when she strolled on the deck with her two girls, nine-year-old Isabel and little Elvira, aged seven. From Dona Isabel, young Hernando began to learn courtly manners and etiquette. The boy from the rough world of Extremadura now had a glimpse of the world of refinement and good taste.

The fleet paused briefly at the Canary Islands for provisions, then sailed on. Almost a month later they sighted gulls flying overhead, a sign that land could be nearby. Soon they made out the shapes of trees on a distant shore. They had reached the green and mountainous island of Dominica, where they anchored to find fresh water and grass for the horses. A party went ashore with kegs and baskets. The errands were completed quickly, and as soon as a priest said Mass on the beach, the commanders were rowed back to their ships. Hernando returned the ladies to the flagship, then obtained permission to go ashore again to search for his friend San Martín, who seemed to be missing.

The search party, worried by fears of native people, hunted in vain as the night wore on. Then, about one o'clock in the morning, San Martín came strolling out of the forest, cheerful and unworried. He had simply taken a walk, had not realized there was any hurry.

Governor Pedrarias, hearing the story, gave a demonstration of the discipline that had made him infamous. The youth, for having returned late, was taken ashore and hanged from a tree.

Afterwards, Hernando helped dig a grave for his friend. It was a memorable lesson not only about his commanding officer, but about life, death, and justice in the New World.

Another week of sailing brought them near the shore of the New World's mainland. The evening before they would disembark, an officer assigned Hernando the task of guarding Dona Isabel and her daughters. He was given a halberd, a battle-ax with the head of a spear at the top; it was his first real weapon.

*One of the customs of the South American Indians was the use of shooting tubes, or blowguns, for hunting.*

The ship rounded a headland, making for the port of Santa María, today in the country of Colombia. The crew dropped anchor when they saw a group of Indians on the shore, men wearing feathered headdresses and armed with bows and arrows.

Three small boats were dispatched to the beach, one of them carrying a copy of a royal document known as the Demand *(Requerimiento)* of the king. All explorers were charged by Spanish law with reading this paper aloud to any native peoples they met.

It said that if the Indians surrendered and accepted the king of Spain as their ruler and Christianity as their religion, no harm would come to them. If they resisted, they would be destroyed. Pedrarias had been ordered "to appeal to the Indians through kind deeds, so that they may view the Christians with love and friendship." The royal Demand had to be read aloud three times, even if the Indians attacked. Since it was read in Spanish, the whole thing was foolish and useless. But the Spaniards were as strict about laws as they were indifferent to justice.

Sixty Spaniards landed on the beach, facing a hundred shouting Indians, their bodies painted and gleaming with coconut oil. Their attack was fierce and immediate, but the Spaniards were armed with a harquebus, a powerful gun lighter and more portable than a cannon. The roar of two shots from the harquebus frightened off the Indians, who had never heard such a weapon.

Pedrarias soon landed with the rest of his soldiers in formation. A scouting party sent inland found no Indians but discovered some deserted huts from which they stole hammocks, fishing nets, and cotton clothing.

The Spaniards cautiously spent the night on the ships, but landed the next morning with a force under command of Pedrarias the Younger, a nephew of the governor. They found three deserted villages and were stealing everything in sight, including small pieces of gold, when battle cries rang out and armed Indians appeared on every side.

De Soto was among the thirty soldiers surrounded, so this was his first battle. The Spaniards now carried several harquebuses, and again gunfire decided the struggle.

The Spaniards lingered a few days on this coast, looting more abandoned villages, finding a few gold ornaments, some emeralds, and a large sapphire. It was fairly good booty, but Hernando saw other things less appealing: there were human legs and arms boiled in cooking pots, and over doorways were skulls set on stakes to ward off strangers. The Spaniards were happy enough to sail away.

By now Hernando had discovered that the New World, or at least this part of it, was not as glorious as the stories he had heard in Spain.

*Cannibalistic Indians in the New World*

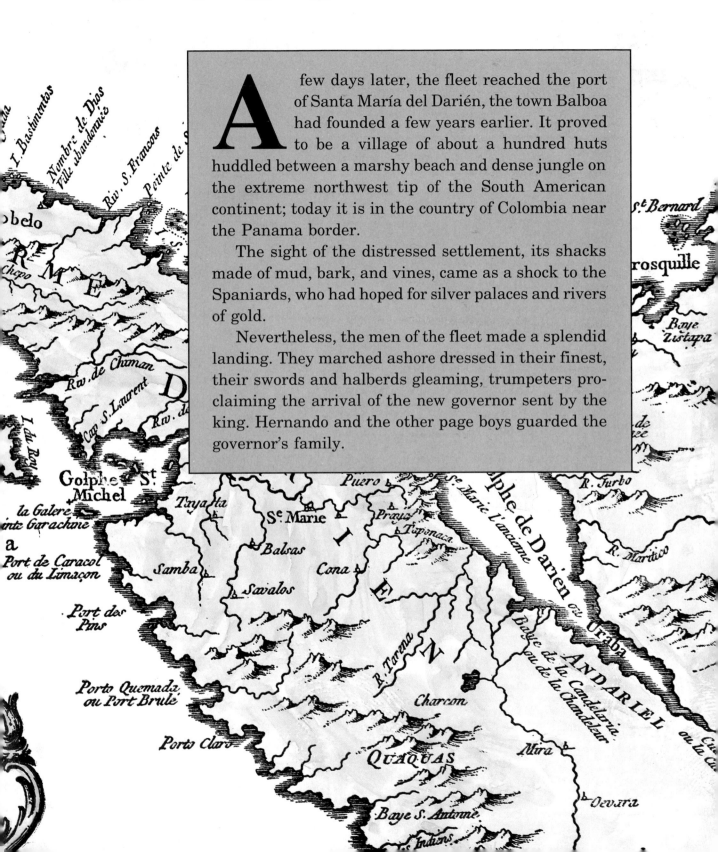

A few days later, the fleet reached the port of Santa María del Darién, the town Balboa had founded a few years earlier. It proved to be a village of about a hundred huts huddled between a marshy beach and dense jungle on the extreme northwest tip of the South American continent; today it is in the country of Colombia near the Panama border.

The sight of the distressed settlement, its shacks made of mud, bark, and vines, came as a shock to the Spaniards, who had hoped for silver palaces and rivers of gold.

Nevertheless, the men of the fleet made a splendid landing. They marched ashore dressed in their finest, their swords and halberds gleaming, trumpeters proclaiming the arrival of the new governor sent by the king. Hernando and the other page boys guarded the governor's family.

Balboa, a brown-haired man with blue eyes in a deeply tanned face, greeted them. He was simply dressed, shod in rope sandals. On his arm was the beautiful Indian princess Anayansi, daughter of a chief who had become Balboa's ally. Living simply and without greed, Balboa was one of the few Spaniards who adapted to the land and people around him.

Governor Pedrarias, jealous and suspicious, hoped to trap Balboa immediately into some admission of misrule. Instead, the great explorer announced his discovery of the Pacific Ocean, then called the South Sea or Southern Ocean. He described peaceful lands he had visited, giving promising news of pearl fisheries and of rivers where a few golden nuggets had been found. The colony, though poor, was in such good order that, for the time being, Pedrarias dared do nothing against Balboa. But he would wait for a chance. Jealousy of the great explorer gnawed at Pedrarias.

Two days later, as Balboa was leaving Governor Pedrarias's house, he greeted young De Soto as a fellow Extremaduran and offered to give him fencing lessons. Thus De Soto first learned swordsmanship from Balboa and quickly proved himself a brilliant pupil.

The Spaniards who had arrived on the fleet soon found themselves in misery. They hated the heat and the insects and feared malaria. A fire in a storehouse burned provisions they had brought from Spain. Starvation loomed before them. The busiest workers in the colony were the grave diggers.

Pedrarias sent one ship of disgruntled Spaniards to Cuba; others he assigned to exploring parties, ordering Balboa on a mission so dangerous that it seemed

*Balboa taking possession of the Pacific Ocean*

doomed from the start. The governor's scheme failed; Balboa returned with even greater honor. Hernando, with the governor's family, moved a few miles away from the settlement to a place said to be more healthful.

His training in arms continued, although Balboa no longer taught him. He drilled with the halberd and lance, meanwhile becoming an outstanding horseman. To Dona Isabel and her daughters he seemed like a member of the family, perhaps a heroic brother. De Soto was popular and known for his cheerful spirits.

Darién had become an informal school for warriors. Constant drill with weapons kept the men from fretting too much about the heat, the discomfort of wearing steel armor in the tropics, the bad food, and swarms of mosquitoes.

*Spanish soldiers on the march through the forests of Central America*

The governor sent one of his lieutenants, Juan de Ayora, with four hundred soldiers to establish new towns. This officer was at first greeted by the natives as a friend of Balboa. He repaid their kindness, however, with looting, hanging, and torture to force them to reveal the hiding places of imaginary treasure.

The powerful Chief Pocorosa captured some Spaniards from Ayora's war party. He avenged their cruelty to his people by tying the captives up, pushing clay funnels down their throats, then pouring molten gold into the funnels. "Choke on gold!" he shouted.

So ended the peace that Balboa had established in Central America. Hernando De Soto seems to have

*Spaniards' mistreatment of the Indians*

learned much from the tragedy. In the future he would try to follow the peaceful ways of Balboa, hoping to gain the friendship of new people. He did not always succeed, but he became one of the few Spanish explorers who understood that force was not always the best tactic.

War blazed along the coast as Governor Pedrarias sought treasure. A new expedition was assigned to Gaspar de Morales with 150 men, among them young Hernando, now on his first real military mission. Dona Isabel and her daughters wished him luck, and he left with her his most valued possession, his copy of *Amadís of Gaul*.

The Spanish expedition moved across the isthmus of Panama led by Indian guides and accompanied by two large, fierce dogs trained for war. The jungle seemed awesome yet fascinating, with gigantic trees such as the balsa and royal palm and birds of brilliant plumage. They saw the grotesque reptiles that the explorer Amerigo Vespucci had described a few years earlier as "snakes with legs." These were, of course, alligators. De Soto and his companions felt uneasy about vampire bats, pythons, and deadly spiders.

At last they reached the magnificent Pacific Ocean, where they were greeted by a friendly Indian chief. Morales, hearing about some nearby islands where pearls were to be found, set off at once in canoes with half his men, including De Soto. The others he left behind among the Indians, which later proved a serious mistake.

As they were crossing to the island, suddenly a gale swept out of the northwest, whipping huge waves to foam, nearly swamping the fragile boats. The Spaniards managed to beat their way to the shore of an inhabited island, but were hardly dry from the storm when shouting Indian warriors charged out of the forest to attack them. As usual, the superior weapons of the Spaniards soon won the day; besides, the Indians were terrified of the savage dogs, never having seen such creatures before. To them, dogs seemed as strange as "snakes with legs" were to Spaniards. Hernando learned another lesson he would remember: the value of attack dogs in battle.

Peace was soon made, and in an exchange of gifts the Spaniards acquired a whole basket full of pearls. One of the pearls was so large that, years later, Dona Isabel would present it as a royal gift to the queen of

*Spaniards believed alligators were snakes with legs.*

*Francisco Pizarro*

Portugal. At last Hernando was seeing some of the fabled wealth of the Indies.

Something even more important happened that same day. The chief led a small group of Spaniards to the summit of a hill. Among them was De Soto and two of his friends, the dauntless warrior Francisco Pizarro and a young nobleman named Hernan Ponce de León. From this hilltop they could see the mainland, the northwest coast of South America. A little to the south, the chief assured them, lay a great kingdom rich in gold. What was this land called?

"*Birú*," the chief said. "*Birú*!"

This was the first time Spaniards had heard of the rich land we now know as Peru, the country where Hernando De Soto would gain fame and riches.

The return of the expedition to Darién was both an adventure and a nightmare. The Indians, formerly gracious, had turned hostile because of the behavior of the Spaniards who had been left behind during the trip to the island. A thousand enraged warriors attacked the Spaniards, almost surrounding them, halting their ferocious onslaught only when darkness fell. The only chance for the Spaniards to survive lay in a surprise counterattack.

Commander Morales assigned half his force to Pizarro, then led the other half to encircle the Indian camp under cover of night. The Spaniards attacked at daybreak, firing harquebuses and unleashing the killer dogs. Soon Spanish armor, steel weapons, and discipline triumphed. Seven hundred Indians lay dead or wounded; the others escaped to the jungle.

*A 1704 map of Panama (Darién) showing population centers that existed at that time*

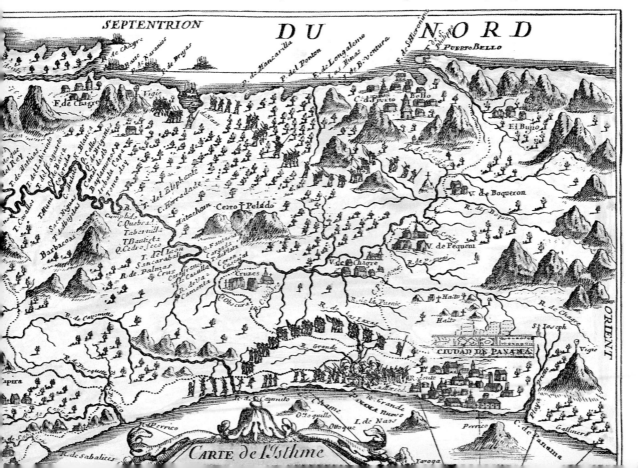

Morales then beheaded nineteen chiefs along with several women and children, saying, "This will inspire fear in all these lands." Perhaps it did; certainly it inspired hatred that would cause bloodshed for generations to come.

Hernando's bravery and skill had been noticed during the expedition. Morales promoted him to captain of lancers. At age seventeen, he was the youngest captain in the Spanish empire. A brilliant future lay ahead of him, yet the months that followed were painful for Hernando. Governor Pedrarias, unable to let his jealousy smolder any longer, brought a list of criminal charges against Balboa. The grievous charge of treason was invented, and Balboa was led to prison in chains. After a mockery of a trial, Pedrarias ordered Balboa's beheading.

*Balboa meeting with Pedrarias*

*Balboa's execution*

The colony was bitterly divided, with no one in a more difficult position than Hernando De Soto. He was Balboa's friend and admirer; he saw injustice about to be committed. Yet Pedrarias was his commander, and he owed all he had to the governor.

To make matters worse, Hernando had fallen in love with Pedrarias's daughter, Isabel, who returned his feelings. To offend the hot-tempered governor was to destroy all his hopes, his future.

Yet on the last night of Balboa's life, Hernando courageously visited him in prison. Then, after the execution, he took the risk of claiming the great explorer's body for a Christian burial on a nearby hillside.

Far more dangerous than his friendship with Balboa was Hernando's falling in love with the governor's daughter. Isabel was of high noble rank on both her father's and her mother's sides of the family. Hernando, despite a promising future, was at present a nobody, an upstart. Yet the two young people were deeply, lastingly in love. Fortunately, no one but the girl's mother, the sympathetic Dona Isabel, saw the truth. Knowing how offended her proud husband would be, she kept the secret, but decided the safe course was to take Isabel home to Spain quickly.

If Hernando made his fortune in the New World, became a figure of wealth and importance, perhaps a marriage with Isabel would become possible. For the present, safety lay in secrecy and distance.

Hernando cannot have failed to realize he was reliving the story of his favorite hero, Amadís, the pure but unknown knight who proved his worth by courage and won a beautiful princess.

In several ways, De Soto was unlike the other famous Spanish captains of his time; but nothing could have been more unusual than his feelings for Isabel. Other adventurers married women they hardly knew in order to gain higher rank or more wealth; some accepted matches their families arranged. Their marriages seemed merely convenient, their wives quite unimportant to them. But such an arrangement would not do for Hernando, who longed to prove himself as a knight and win a high-born lady through valor.

In June 1520, Dona Isabel and her daughters sailed for Spain. Young Isabel had already given Hernando a small gold cross he wore beneath his armor. Now she left him a small prayer book in which she had written, "I will wait for you." Since it was dangerous for her to hand him the book herself, a friend delivered it after her ship was safely at sea.

*Panama City as it appeared in the 1850s, almost three hundred years after Pedrarias founded it*

Meanwhile, Governor Pedrarias had established a new town that is now Panama City on the Pacific, the first European settlement on the western coast of the Americas. He seized three ships that Balboa had been building and resolved to send exploring parties to find treasure.

In this the governor enjoyed some success, snatching gold and pearls from the Indians; but the cost was terrible in suffering and loss of life, including the lives of many Spaniards.

De Soto's share of the booty was not large, but he saved every sliver of gold for his future. With other officers, he explored much of the Central American isthmus and was among the first to sail across broad Lake Nicaragua.

*Lake Nicaragua*

His life was filled with constant peril and fighting, with some of the struggles against Spaniards, not Indians. Certain of his countrymen had set out on their own to seek riches and so became outlaws.

In his first battle against such men, De Soto surrounded the camp of a marauder named González under cover of darkness. De Soto and his men attacked fiercely and were easily winning a victory when González cried out, "Señor Captain, peace, peace in the emperor's name."

Hernando, still believing in the rules of chivalry he had learned in books, ordered the fighting stopped. "Never let it be said that I attacked a defeated enemy or questioned a gentleman's word," he is said to have told his men.

*Hernando Cortés*

The surrender was a trick. In a few hours, a large force of men González had been waiting for arrived to overpower De Soto's company. González took not only De Soto's sword, but his leather purse with all his hard-won savings. Three days later De Soto was released from captivity with his sword returned to him. González kept Hernando's gold. This lesson in treachery was among the hardest Hernando learned in Panama.

Word of Hernando Cortés's conquest of Mexico's Aztec empire reached Panama, and the Spanish army buzzed with tales of golden cities with silver streets. Other kingdoms, as rich as Mexico, must be hidden somewhere! A new spirit of hope and determination sprang up among the soldiers, and De Soto was as eager as the others.

Meanwhile, De Soto had decided there might be a better way of acquiring gold than stealing it from Indians. With his two closest friends, Hernan Ponce de León and Francisco Campañón, he formed a mining company in Nicaragua. Indeed, this venture soon proved far more profitable than the business of attacking impoverished villages.

For a time Hernando was contented. He took part in tournaments, proving himself the best rider and lancer in the army. Everyone, it seemed, liked the tall, handsome captain with his merry laugh and warm smile. He wore a small beard now in the fashion of the day, a black point below his chin.

Then tragedy and greater wealth came to De Soto at the same time. His friend Campañón died of a sudden illness, leaving his share of the mining company to be divided between Hernando and Ponce de León.

De Soto was tired of the New World, disgusted by the endless schemes and plots of officers and government officials, angered by the tyranny and cruelty of the governor. He considered returning to Spain with the gold he now owned. Perhaps it was enough for him to propose marriage to Isabel. Although still a young man, he had survived more than enough adventures for a lifetime.

Just at that time, he heard again of an almost unknown kingdom to the south, the land he had glimpsed long ago from the hilltop of an island. The thought of it set his mind and heart racing.

Hernando De Soto was suddenly drawn by a new challenge, a country called Peru.

*The Black River of Nauta, Peru*

# Chapter 4
## The Gold of the Incas

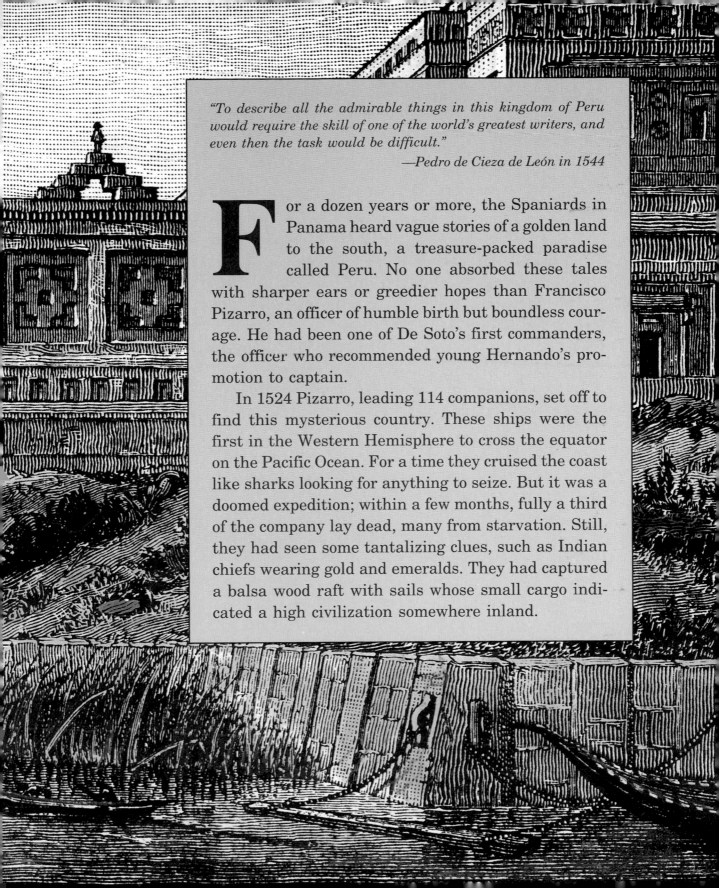

> *"To describe all the admirable things in this kingdom of Peru would require the skill of one of the world's greatest writers, and even then the task would be difficult."*
>
> —*Pedro de Cieza de León in 1544*

For a dozen years or more, the Spaniards in Panama heard vague stories of a golden land to the south, a treasure-packed paradise called Peru. No one absorbed these tales with sharper ears or greedier hopes than Francisco Pizarro, an officer of humble birth but boundless courage. He had been one of De Soto's first commanders, the officer who recommended young Hernando's promotion to captain.

In 1524 Pizarro, leading 114 companions, set off to find this mysterious country. These ships were the first in the Western Hemisphere to cross the equator on the Pacific Ocean. For a time they cruised the coast like sharks looking for anything to seize. But it was a doomed expedition; within a few months, fully a third of the company lay dead, many from starvation. Still, they had seen some tantalizing clues, such as Indian chiefs wearing gold and emeralds. They had captured a balsa wood raft with sails whose small cargo indicated a high civilization somewhere inland.

Pizarro tried again, landing on an island called Gallo, where he waited for more forces to come from Panama. But when a ship finally arrived, it brought an order from Pedrarias: Pizarro and his men were to return.

Francisco Pizarro assembled all the soldiers and sailors on the beach. Facing them all, he challenged their courage. He drew his sword, marked a line in the sand, and then, in a scene now famous in history, dared the men to choose sides. "Return to Panama and live in poverty, or follow me to Peru and become rich!"

Thirteen men (some historians say sixteen) crossed the line to join Pizarro—certainly a modest beginning for the leader's vast ambitions.

*Pizarro challenging his men to cross the line and follow him*

In the next months, these adventurers learned still more about the great kingdom hidden behind the mountain peaks that towered toward the clouds in the distance. Although they found some gold objects, beautiful pottery, and woven cloth, they were too small a group to press on.

Pizarro went to Spain with his evidence of Peruvian riches and succeeded in winning some support from the king. Then he quickly returned to the New World seeking more men and supplies. The officer he wanted most was Hernando De Soto. Pizarro valued De Soto so highly that he tempted him with the position of lieutenant general—second-in-command.

De Soto hesitated. Then Governor Pedrarias suddenly died, leaving Hernando free to choose his future. The challenge of exploring the south grew irresistible. De Soto sold his property in Central America, bought two ships, and recruited about a hundred men. He also invested in fifty horses and large quantities of food, arms, and tools. Among his few personal belongings, he packed his worn copy of *Amadís of Gaul*. The perfect knight would again be his inspiration.

Pizarro, on the coast of South America, greeted Hernando joyfully. De Soto no doubt felt a good deal less happy about their reunion. Pizarro's men, numbering less than two hundred, were worried and discouraged. Also, he learned that Pizarro had deceived him about the rank he was to hold—not lieutenant general, Pizarro confessed, because he had already given that post to his own brother, Hernando Pizarro. A description of this brother has come down to us: "Tall and fat, with a gross tongue and full lips, the tip of his nose overladen with flesh and highly colored." Those who knew him described him as arrogant.

Nevertheless, the red-nosed brother was to have the position promised to De Soto. Pizarro soothed De Soto's annoyance by assuring him that De Soto would actually exercise the power of second-in-command, would have everything but the title.

Pizarro's lie, told to lure De Soto to Peru, was typical of the man's character. Coarse, brutal, and uneducated, Pizarro looms in history as one of the more detestable figures of his time.

De Soto was just over thirty years old when he arrived on the South American coast, and Pizarro was about twenty-five years older, although his exact birth date is uncertain. Both men came from impoverished Extremadura; both were daring fighters seeking fortunes. But that is all they had in common.

Pizarro and De Soto sailed a short distance to make a landing at an Indian town called Tumbez. This time the natives attacked while the men were still on rafts or in the water. After three desperate tries, Pizarro brought his small army ashore.

De Soto, always cautious, led a column of soldiers on a fighting and scouting expedition to make sure the area was safe. Soon the Indians charged from ambush, forcing De Soto into a short, sharp battle he quickly won. Talking later to a captured chieftain, De Soto learned of the magnificent Inca kingdom high in the Andes Mountains.

The word "Inca" confused the Spaniards when they first heard it, for it had several meanings. The Incas were once a small tribe who conquered all their neighbors, and so "Inca" came to mean a ruler or nobleman. When they said "the Inca" or "the great Inca," it meant the emperor of all these people of the Andes.

The Incas proudly called their empire the Four Corners of the World. This vast region covered what today is Peru, Ecuador, and parts of Colombia and Bolivia. In size, it was as large as the whole southwestern United States today, the states of Texas, Arizona, New Mexico, and California combined. Six million Indians lived in this region, governed by a king who claimed to be the child of the sun itself. Inca civilization was advanced in agriculture, engineering, and crafts.

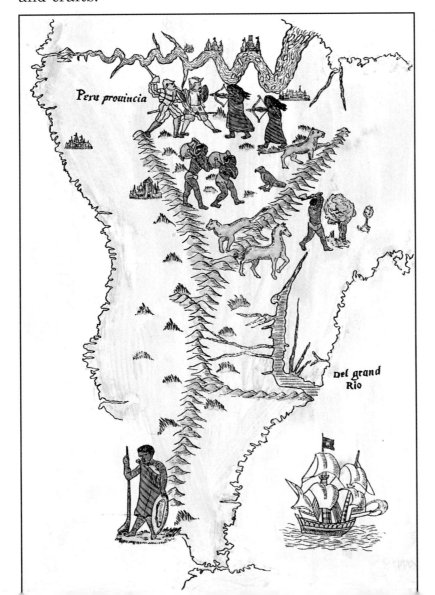

*This map of South America, drawn in 1544, shows the province of Peru in the northwest corner*

Peru prouincia

Del grand Rio

*Inca king Huayna Capac*

The empire had two capitals: Cuzco, today in Peru, was the older city and center for the southern part of the nation. Quito, now the capital of Ecuador, was the center for the north. The Incas built fine roads, had relay services for rapid messages, and even sent mail on the backs of llamas, those curious animals that carry burdens up to fifty pounds (twenty-three kilograms).

About the year 1450 there was born a ruler, Huayna Capac, who firmly united and controlled the empire. Growing old and sensing death, he divided the country into two kingdoms, the northern part for his favorite son, Atahualpa. Another son, Prince Huascar, would inherit the southern lands with Cuzco as the capital.

King Huayna Capac had already heard of the first exploring parties of Spaniards along the coast when he died, but no one at his court paid much attention

*Cuzco in 1556, after Spaniards had taken it over*

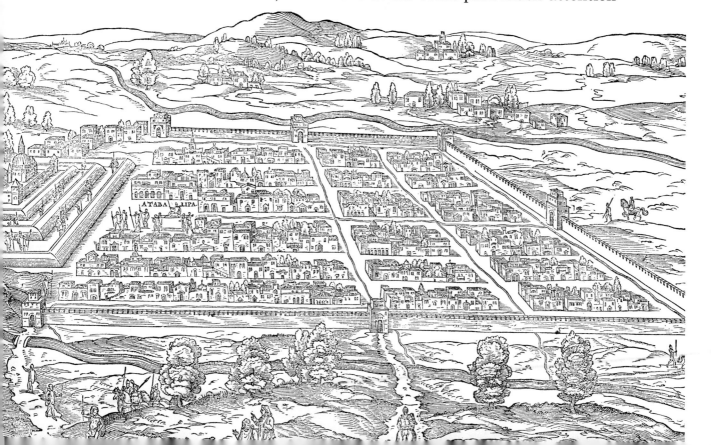

to the doings of the strangers. The old king's magnificent funeral had to be conducted, his embalmed body carried in state more than 1,000 miles (1,609 kilometers) along the twisting but beautiful road from Quito to Cuzco.

For the next few years, while the Spaniards were gathering their information and their forces, there was peace between the two kingdoms in Peru.

Then a civil war broke out. King Atahualpa won victory after victory for the northern forces; soon Huascar, who had ruled in the south, was captured and imprisoned in a fortress. Atahualpa, almost the same age as Hernando De Soto, retired to rest after his triumph and to recover from a wound. It was then that news came of the strange men with white skins who were arriving on his shore in what seemed to be floating houses.

*The murder of Huascar by order of Atahualpa*

Two great civilizations, one Spanish and the other Peruvian, were about to meet, and one would be destroyed forever.

Francisco Pizarro moved into action. He left a small guard with sick and wounded soldiers at Tumbez, then set out with a column of one hundred men to scout the lowlands. De Soto, with seventy soldiers, would move straight toward the mountains, if possible reaching the Royal Highway they had heard of.

For Hernando it was a strange expedition. He quickly reached the Royal Highway and advanced along it with no opposition, passing strongholds and temples. Herds of llamas, grazing in meadows, seemed peaceful as herds of sheep, and the Spaniards were astonished at the sight of these strange creatures. In the distance loomed the majestic Andes, far higher than any peaks the Spaniards had ever beheld.

People in small villages offered ample food and marveled at the Spaniards' beards, since their own men were beardless. A few even asked the soldiers to bare their chests so they might see if these strange newcomers were truly white all over.

Yet the scene was not as harmless as it appeared. Hernando suspected an ambush and kept his men on the alert. He was proven right when out of the twilight armed warriors burst upon them, yelling and brandishing stone weapons, shooting arrows, and hurling darts.

The Spanish harquebuses exploded with deadly fire, and horses and lancers charged. After a few minutes the enemy fled in disorder, vanishing into the darkness.

Hernando, taking some prisoners with him, rejoined Pizarro the next day, and the commanders made

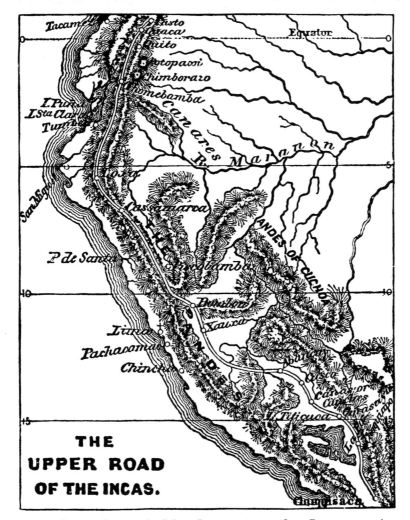

THE
UPPER ROAD
OF THE INCAS.

*The Incas' "highway" through the Andes: Quito is in the north, just south of the equator, and Cuzco is in the south near the 13-degree point.*

their plans for a bold advance on the Inca empire. Pizarro would lead 160 soldiers toward a place called Cajamarca, where King Atahualpa was thought to be resting and recovering after his victory in the civil war. De Soto, with a dozen horsemen, would ride ahead to scout for Indian troops.

De Soto quickly reached the highway and there was met by messengers from the king, a group of magnificently dressed Indian nobles. Their leader was a man the Spaniards called Long Ears because his earlobes were stretched out of shape by the weight of gold earrings the size of a man's fist.

The richness of Long Ears' costume amazed the Spaniards: a beautiful mantle woven of a dozen colors, with gold on his cuffs, in his hair, and around his ankles. They especially noticed a large gold medallion hanging against his chest with a carved picture of his own face. If this was a messenger, even a noble one, what must the king be like?

Hernando led Long Ears back to the place where Pizarro had camped for the night, and it was quickly arranged that Pizarro would meet King Atahualpa in Cajamarca.

De Soto, who would be at the head of the march, made careful preparations for a journey through steep mountains. He knew he was about to enter a strange new world concealed by the lofty, snow-capped peaks. But he could not have imagined how magnificent this world would be, how different from anything that he, or any other European, had ever known.

They moved through rocky foothills, then ascended craggy slopes. There the narrow, twisting trails were so high they could look down on clouds and upward at the eternal snows of the peaks. Streams of icy water plunged downward over boulders, making the slippery ground risky for the horses. The Spaniards shivered in the thin mountain air while the horses panted. De Soto, with forty men in the vanguard, blazed a path for the others.

De Soto looked up at sheer cliffs where Indian sentinels stood, realizing the whole Spanish army could be destroyed by a few warriors starting an avalanche of stones. All the soldiers suspected they were climbing into a fatal trap. Francisco Pizarro joined De Soto at the head of the column, leaving his brother to urge on the rear guard.

They spent one uneasy night in an abandoned fortress built of huge stone blocks cleverly fitted together to form walls without mortar.

Once they had passed the huge spine of the mountains and began to descend, the journey became easier. Another messenger from King Atahualpa met them, offering a drink made of corn milk served in golden cups. The Spaniards could hardly bear to return their cups when they finished drinking. Pizarro sent the warmest and friendliest greetings to the king. He would visit him soon.

But it was not as soon as Pizarro expected. It took seven more days before they descended into the green and fertile valley of Cajamarca. The people who lived there, dressed in dark clothing brightened by red embroidery, tended their herds of llamas and carefully avoided looking at the newcomers.

*Pizarro and his men scrambling up the steep mountain passes of the Andes*

The valley offered a startling view. At one end stood a city, its streets lined with white houses and a large open square, or plaza, in the center. Far away, in the opposite direction, thin clouds of steam rose from natural hot springs. Farther on stretched row after row of white cotton tents—thousands of them. This was the enormous camp of King Atahualpa and his army.

De Soto and Pizarro rode into the silent city and found not a soul in the streets or buildings; it stood deserted, ghostly. The Spaniards set up their quarters in buildings on the main square.

Pizarro, worried about what might happen when night fell, immediately sent an envoy to King Atahualpa, choosing his best officer—Hernando De Soto. So Hernando became the first man from the outside world to meet this god-king who was revered as the Child of the Sun. De Soto took with him fifteen horsemen carrying banners and a trumpeter to sound shrill salutes through the hushed valley.

Suddenly rain and hail began to pelt the horsemen as the sky darkened and thunder rolled over the mountain landscape, resounding from the cliffs. Here was a scene as eerie and mysterious as anything in *Amadís of Gaul*.

At the Inca camp the greatest nobles waited, gorgeously attired in robes adorned with opals, pearls, and gold. Under a roof, sitting on a low stool, was Atahualpa himself, the supreme ruler, the Child of the Sun. De Soto's cavalry swept to the first row of noblemen, trumpets blaring. There De Soto dismounted, doffing his plumed helmet as he moved calmly and courteously toward Atahualpa until the two were close together.

*Atahualpa, the Inca king*

Atahualpa ignored De Soto's greeting, deliberately staring to one side, pretending not to see the astonishing sight of gleaming armor, helmets, and horses. The king was about thirty-six years old at the time, four years older than Hernando. Attired in his tall golden crown with a tassel of red wool, he seemed a personage of immense dignity.

De Soto respectfully invited the king to visit the Spaniards, but the king seemed not to listen to the interpreters. There was no reply, no sign, until at last a nobleman said, "It is well." Then came an even longer silence.

The quiet was broken by the clatter of hooves and armor. Hernando Pizarro, the commander's stout and red-nosed brother, galloped onto the scene with cavalry reinforcements.

"My lord," said De Soto, "this is the brother of my commander who will repeat the invitation to our camp."

Again, after what seemed an eternity of silence laden with danger, Atahualpa said to Long Ears, his interpreter, "Tell your captain that I am fasting until tomorrow. Tell him also he may repair to the buildings on the square where you are staying. After that I will give further orders."

Atahualpa looked at De Soto's spirited mare with open curiosity. De Soto realized instantly how to end this strange interview. Leaping into the saddle, he put the mare through her paces, displaying the skill and balance that had made him famous as a rider. Horse and rider moved in swift circles, Hernando dropping the reins, guiding her only with the pressure of his knees. She charged, reared, retreated a few steps on her hind legs, then De Soto had her clear a fence in a single astonishing leap. He finally brought her to a halt so close to the king that foam from the horse's mouth fell on the hem of the royal mantle. Some of the nobles cringed and drew back a few steps, but Atahualpa held his position, fearless and majestic. Later that night he sentenced to death all the nobles who had betrayed their fear in front of the strangers.

The Spaniards took leave with great ceremony just as darkness was falling. When they reached their own headquarters a council was assembled to hear reports and plan strategy.

The Spaniards numbered 170 men. Atahualpa had a force of about thirty thousand warriors, perhaps half of them already in the valley, the rest on the way. The plight of the Spaniards might have seemed hopeless. Yet, Pizarro knew how Cortés had first won power in Mexico a few years earlier: by seizing and holding Moctezuma, emperor of the Aztecs. Pizarro now announced his plan to seize Atahualpa during the royal visit the next day.

All the assembled officers agreed except De Soto, who felt such tactics were dishonorable. Attack the king's headquarters openly, he urged. Or, if that seemed impossible, make certain that no harm came to Atahualpa as a prisoner. They should be open and honest about their demands and intentions.

Pizarro agreed instantly, guaranteeing the king's safety. De Soto, who usually believed the best about his countrymen, believed Pizarro's promise.

The next day, about noon, a huge army of Incas moved slowly along the road toward the Spanish headquarters. In the vanguard were scores of musicians and dancers, then a company of warriors armed with clubs tipped with copper spikes. (Copper was the only metal the Incas knew how to use for weaponry.) The mass of the army carried spears with nooses attached, designed for either killing or capturing an enemy.

Next, hundreds of servants moved into view, sweepers and cleaners to remove the least leaf or pebble for the royal passage of the Child of the Sun. The king arrived last with his glittering noblemen decked with gold to dazzle Spanish eyes. They carried Atahualpa on a litter adorned with a rainbow of plumes from parrots and toucans. He sat on a throne of solid gold.

Just before reaching the plaza, the king halted the column, seized by uncertainty. Then, in response to an urgent entreaty from Pizarro, he entered the plaza with five thousand men.

Not a Spaniard was to be seen in the great square; all lay hidden in the surrounding buildings. Then a lone Spanish priest emerged from a doorway, followed by an interpreter. For a moment he and the king talked. The priest handed Atahualpa a Bible, which the king glanced at, then hurled to the ground.

"Blasphemy!" shouted the priest, raising his arms. This was the signal for the Spanish attack. Pizarro leaped from a doorway waving a handkerchief. "Charge!" he shouted, and the Spaniards rushed from hiding, giving the battle cry of Spain, "Santiago! Santiago!"

Horses galloped among the unarmed nobles, who were ridden down, trampled, and stabbed with lances. Pizarro and twenty men seized the king, while harquebuses roared, hailing death upon the guards. Panic filled the square, panic so wild that the plaza

*Pizarro and a priest standing before Atahualpa*

*Inca warriors, from an early Peruvian painting*

walls crumbled under the pressure of bodies, collapsing, freeing thousands who fled in terror. In half an hour the massacre was over; countless Indians lay dead on the ground, their king a captive in one of the houses. De Soto returned with his cavalry, sounding a trumpet signal that all was safe, the enemy defeated. The Spaniards had suffered only a single wound: Pizarro himself had a gash in one hand.

It was the sixteenth of November, 1532. In a sense, this was the first day of a new world for the people of South America.

The Spaniards looted the dead bodies and the Incas' encampment the next morning, but De Soto did not join the robbery. He talked to Atahualpa, trying to teach the king a few words of Spanish, while hoping to learn the history and customs of Peru.

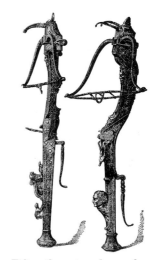

*Fifteenth-century harquebuses*

*Atahualpa's subjects bringing in gold and silver for ransom*

During the months that followed, Atahualpa was closely guarded while the Spaniards scoured the country for booty and for signs of revolt. They detected no signs of rebellion, no massing of an Indian army. The Incas were so shocked by the imprisonment of their ruler, a king they revered as a god, that the country was paralyzed by despair and confusion.

King Atahualpa came to realize that gold and silver were the only things that Pizarro and his men craved. He offered to ransom himself, offering Pizarro enough gold to fill the room where he was imprisoned from floor to ceiling. "I will also fill the next room twice over with silver. This will be done within two months, then you will set me free."

Pizarro gave his word at once. Yes, the king would have his freedom. After all, this was more gold than any ruler in the world had ever been able to collect, and promises were cheap to Pizarro.

Week after week, gold and silver poured in from every corner of the Inca empire—cups, pitchers, bowls, and plates. The Spaniards gazed on it with greed and astonishment. The room to be filled was twenty feet (six meters) long and seventeen feet (five meters) wide; Atahualpa promised that it would be stacked with the precious metal to a height of nine feet (2.7 meters). It seemed impossible to Pizarro. Was there really so much gold in all the world?

It kept pouring in, load after load, gold in bags on the backs of men and llamas. The beautiful golden objects, masterpieces of the art of goldsmithing, were melted into gold bars so the Spaniards could divide them and carry them off more easily.

*Ceremonial gold knife made in Peru before the arrival of the Spaniards*

Meanwhile, another party of Spaniards had arrived from Panama and were demanding a share of the booty. When the gold was finally divided up, Hernando De Soto was one of the richest men of Spain.

The royal ransom had been paid. Atahualpa was demanding his freedom, and De Soto urged Pizarro to keep the promise quickly and honorably.

Pizarro, however, had other plans, though he did not dare to carry them out while De Soto was present. Pretending to have heard about a rebellion in a distant region, Pizarro sent De Soto on a long journey to handle it. The next day Pizarro brought Atahualpa to trial on a dozen invented charges. Doubtless Pizarro was afraid that Atahualpa, if released, would raise an Indian army and drive the Spaniards from Peru. This would put an end to Pizarro's looting. However, alive but in prison, the king would be living evidence of Pizarro's having broken a solemn promise.

Even Pizarro seemed ashamed of his own deed. Instead of holding the execution in daylight, as was the custom, he ordered Atahualpa strangled in darkness. The king died bravely, showing no fear, walking majestically toward the execution stake, his head held high, the scene lit by flickering torches.

De Soto returned soon afterwards, furious. Not only had the report of a rebellion proven false, but he heard of the king's execution while still on the road.

In an angry confrontation with Pizarro, Hernando announced that he was leaving for Spain, that the death of Atahualpa had shamed all Spaniards. But returning to Spain seemed impossible even to De Soto. Civil war was breaking out in Peru. For two years Hernando practically lived in the saddle, galloping across the country from one battle to another.

*Gold zodiac found at Cuzco, worn as a breastplate by an Inca ruler*

*Pizarro orders the execution of Atahualpa*

Pizarro named De Soto captain general of the expedition to reach the great capital at Cuzco, heart of the Inca empire. It was thus that Hernando discovered the mountain passes that led to this fabled city. He was reported to be the first horseman to cross the swaying bridges the Indians had woven of willow strands to span gorges and chasms at dizzying heights in the Andes.

De Soto, after bloody and hard-fought struggles, succeeded in entering the capital. Eventually he was named governor of Cuzco, becoming even richer in gold and fame. But he longed to leave Peru; Isabel was waiting, and his adventures seemed over.

When he sailed for Spain in 1535, he could certainly not have supposed that his greatest achievements, and the most dangerous ones, still lay ahead.

*An Inca bridge made of woven plant fibers*

# Chapter 5
# A New Land Beckons

Hernando De Soto's triumphant return to Spain seems like the ending of a knightly legend or a fairy tale where the prince finds the princess, dangers are put behind, and "they all lived happily ever after."

Hernando married Isabel, now even more beautiful as a woman than she had been as a girl, and set up a splendid residence. He had become so famous that the king himself, Charles V, wanted to meet the daring young captain and summoned him to the royal palace. The monarch, it turned out, needed to borrow gold from De Soto to help meet the expenses of Spain's endless European conflicts. De Soto said he was honored by the request; certainly he could afford it.

For a time Hernando seemed content to bask in his new honors and wealth. Yet, throughout this period of his life, he kept in close touch with the New World. Old friends and acquaintances returning from Peru or Panama brought him news.

Soon he began to hear more about a vast, unexplored region called Florida. Pizarro, with powerful help from De Soto, had conquered Peru; Cortés had subdued Mexico. But what of the lands to the north, this unmapped part of the world known as Florida? Could other, even richer kingdoms be hidden in its wilderness? De Soto began to wonder.

The mysterious Florida that De Soto was thinking about was far larger than the state we call Florida today. The name vaguely meant all the New World north of Mexico, all that is the United States and Canada today.

A few daring Spaniards had landed on its southern coast: Juan Ponce de León, Lucas Vázquez de Ayllón, and Panfilo de Narzáez. None of them had learned much about what lay beyond the palm-fringed shore. The Indians were fierce, the forests tangled and forbidding. So the huge land remained a blank space on the map of the world.

While Hernando was pondering these matters, another famous explorer arrived in Seville. This was Alvar Núñez Cabeza de Vaca, a tall, lean, deeply sunburned adventurer who told astonishing stories. Ten years earlier, Cabeza de Vaca had been one of six hundred men who sailed for Florida. And he was one of only four who returned alive. After being shipwrecked on what is now the coast of Texas, he had wandered through the American Southwest, the country north of Cortés's Mexico. Gold was to be found in these rich lands, great cities and palaces. The explorer became a regular visitor at Hernando's house, much to the annoyance of Isabel, who did not want dreams of distant lands rekindled in her husband's mind.

From others Hernando heard stories of mangrove swamps and coral reefs, of lands rich for farming, of the beautiful islands where Spaniards had already established prosperous settlements.

Soon the allure of Florida became irresistible to Hernando. He presented his petition to the king, who was delighted that such a hero as De Soto wished to go forth to find even greater wealth for the Spanish crown. So pleased was the monarch that he not only granted Hernando's requests, but raised him to a higher rank of nobility and named him the new governor of the colony of Cuba.

So Hernando De Soto was off on his next and greatest adventure, and in this he seems to have had the full support of his wife. Isabel was, after all, a soldier's daughter who had spent important years of her life in strange lands. And she would not be separated from her husband, for Isabel intended to accompany him at least as far as Cuba.

Spaniards flocked to join Hernando's new undertaking. A spirit of wildness, a total disregard for caution, seemed to sweep through the country. Men of all classes sold everything they owned to plunge into a perilous and unknown future.

De Soto bought ships and recruited both soldiers and settlers for the new lands. Gold was very much in Hernando's mind, of course; but he saw beyond the notion of a treasure hunt. The original plan had been for an expedition of five hundred men. Now it appeared that a thousand were going. De Soto collected money from them for passage, but he also spent most of his own fortune on ships and equipment. His mother-in-law, Dona Isabel, offered her jewels, a contribution that De Soto gallantly refused.

*Coral is beautiful but can gash a hole in the hull of a ship.*

Thirty ships set sail on an April morning in 1538. De Soto strode up the gangplank of his flagship, elegantly dressed. Beside him, clad in a sweeping gown of scarlet brocade, was his beautiful wife. Then slowly the largest, most powerful fleet that ever voyaged to the Indies weighed anchor and moved slowly toward the Atlantic. Hernando watched the shore of Spain gradually fade in the distance as he embarked now on a new adventure, another new world.

Almost two months later, at the end of May and just two sailing days off Cuba, the fleet separated according to plans made in Spain. Twenty ships, called the Mexican Fleet, turned their prows toward Veracruz, the Mexican port where they would deliver supplies, settlers, and reinforcements. De Soto, with the ten remaining vessels, continued safely to Cuba.

Once ashore, De Soto lost no time in training his army. The cavalry, grown now to four hundred men on horseback, had especially hard exercises. Hernando knew from experience how important they would be in any battles that lay ahead. Before long he moved his headquarters to a beautiful bay on the opposite end of the island, to a village we now know as Havana. From here he sent two small ships to explore and map the nearby coast of Florida.

Two months later, his scouting vessels returned with maps and with two Indians who were beginning to learn Spanish. De Soto wanted interpreters as well as all possible information about Florida before he launched his operation. He told his scouts to return to Florida.

As he prepared to leave, Hernando considered his duties as governor of Cuba. Who would act in his absence? Instead of one of his officers, he chose his

*De Soto's expedition landing at Tampa Bay*

wife as acting governor who would rule Cuba in his place. Thus Isabel became the first European woman to hold power and a high office in the Americas.

Hernando sailed for Florida on May 18 with nine ships carrying his army and their arms, tools, and provisions, their dogs of war, and their domestic animals. Altogether there were 350 horses. Twelve days later, they landed on the Florida coast near a village whose chief was a man named Uscita. Hernando went ashore attended by drummers, trumpeters, and soldiers carrying banners. The officers gleamed in their polished armor as they waded ashore at a place they named Bayo Espirito Santo. This may have been what we call Tampa Bay today.

Hernando De Soto, in a solemn ceremony, planted a flag and claimed all this land for the king of Spain. To modern eyes, this scene is astonishing in its arrogance. A handful of men were announcing their possession of a vast continent of which they had seen only the shore and which was already inhabited by several million native people. But however boastful the claim, this was truly a remarkable moment, the first steps of De Soto's great march through the wilderness.

De Soto's claim was soon challenged. At about three o'clock the next morning, while half the Spaniards were sleeping on the beach, hundreds of warriors suddenly leaped from behind trees and bushes, yelling as they brandished hatchets of flint decked with feathers.

These were stalwart Indians who shaved their heads, leaving only a topknot of hair to hold eagle feathers. Arrows, flint-tipped, hailed down on the Spaniards, who flung themselves against the attackers, meanwhile sounding trumpets to warn men sleeping on shipboard that help might be needed.

Harquebuses roared, horsemen plunged along the beach wielding deadly lances. Such unexpected resistance surprised the Indians, who quickly vanished into the night. Several Spanish soldiers and one horse died of arrow wounds.

Reinforcements were needed. The remaining horses on ships were brought ashore at dawn. Eventually these became the ancestors of almost all the horses that settlers found in the North American forests and plains. The same is true of the dogs and pigs De Soto unloaded. Some eventually became wild and their descendants were discovered many years later.

De Soto lost little time in beginning his explorations. Some writers have claimed that he was simply on a treasure hunt, another Spanish adventurer looking for gold.

Doubtless this was true of many of De Soto's companions. But Hernando himself had little need of more riches. Apart from his simple love of discovery, he now hoped to open up broad new lands for Spanish settlement.

His men scouted the bay, then began moving northward, soon reaching an Indian village called Ocita. The tribal leader, Chief Hirrihigua, had fled at news of the Spaniards' approach. He had suffered from the cruelty of a Spanish force that had tried to land in Florida a few years before. His nose had been cut off and some of his men lost their hands, hacked off by Spanish axes.

De Soto sent gifts to the chief and tried to explain by messengers that there were good Spaniards and bad Spaniards, just as there must be good and bad among Hirrihigua's own people. His offer of friendship was spurned. De Soto would soon learn that all native people who had met up with Spaniards earlier hated them.

De Soto learned that a Spaniard from the earlier expedition was living not far away as a captive with a chief named Mococo, who was famed for kindness. De Soto sent a company of horsemen to rescue his countryman.

After riding some distance, the Spaniards came upon a group of warriors, perhaps two dozen, wearing red war paint and feathers in their tufts of hair. One of them, carrying a bow and arrows and wearing a loincloth, came running forward.

*De Soto coming upon Juan Ortiz*

"In the name of God and the Blessed Virgin, do not kill me!" he shouted, falling to his knees and making the sign of the cross. "I am a Christian!"

Thus they found Juan Ortiz, a Spaniard who had lived for years among the Indians, suffering terrible cruelty until he had found refuge with Chief Mococo.

Chief Hirrihigua would never forgive or approach the Spaniards, but Mococo came to call three days later, bringing his highest-ranking men. This was a friendly meeting with careful courtesy on both sides. Mococo stayed about a week, bringing food and offering his new friends any aid he could give.

About this time the Spaniards were astonished to find in their midst a Spanish woman, Francisca Hinestrosa. Not wanting to be separated from her husband, she had persuaded him to lend her his clothing, and so she came disguised as a man. The couple were in fear of De Soto's wrath, but instead Hernando was amused. He assigned Francisca to work as a cook and a nurse.

Hernando was ready to move farther inland, but first he sent seven of his ships back to Cuba with messages for the Spanish king and letters and gifts for his wife. Meanwhile, De Soto made every effort to befriend the Indians. Any captured native was quickly sent home enriched with presents. But nothing impressed Hirrihigua.

*The De Soto expedition making camp in Florida*

*Flamingos*

*A Florida cypress tree*

On June 15, two weeks after their landing, Hernando left Ocita to begin his exploration of North American lands. They moved past the village of Chief Mococo, then into the territory of hostile people, quickly learning to stay close together in the line of march. Stragglers would be killed by Indians. Hernando lost fourteen men on this first leg of his journey.

They reached the higher ground of northern Florida, richer land with groves of beautiful trees, and were delighted at the sight of herons and flamingos, of lacy moss and tall cypresses.

The town of Ocala proved to have about six hundred houses. These dwellings that early Spanish writers called "houses" were probably what we call

*A Florida Indian's home, with thatched roof*

"wigwams" today—round or oval huts made of bark, wood, thatch, and mud plaster. Later they saw many different kinds of dwellings, some made of logs and a few big enough to be meeting halls.

The houses of Ocala were empty, but food had been left behind, so De Soto camped here to rest the men and animals. A few days later, an Indian of huge stature appeared, the chief himself. De Soto greeted him courteously and asked for some men to help build a bridge across a wide river. The chief graciously agreed and went with De Soto to inspect a spot on the riverbank. De Soto cautiously wore his armor, which proved wise when two hundred Indians burst from thickets shooting arrows and uttering war cries.

After the attack was repulsed, the chief protested that it was not his fault. His men had acted against his orders.

The Spaniards built the bridge quickly, then moved on into what today is Alachua County, to the present-day site of Gainsville, Florida. Vitacucho, the chief here, was a wizard who tried black magic against the newcomers, but his spells failed. He consented to meet De Soto, seemed friendly, and offered to accompany Hernando through his territory, staying constantly at his side.

One day Ortiz, the Spaniard who had lived among the Indians, overheard a plot to destroy these intruders by ambush. Thus, De Soto was forewarned. As expected, Vitacucho gave De Soto an invitation, almost a dare, to watch ten thousand warriors parade in a meadow not far away. De Soto agreed at once. "My men will march side by side with your men," he said.

Vitacucho and De Soto were at the head of the column when they emerged from the forest upon an open plain. There, indeed, were ten thousand warriors painted and armed for battle. Vitacucho gave a signal, his hatchet raised in the air, and suddenly battle was raging across the plain. De Soto leaped upon his horse Aceituno, hefted a lance, and plunged into the thick of the fray. It was for good reason that De Soto was famed as the best lancer in the army; it took only a few minutes to rout Vitacucho's men.

The battle swept this way and that, harquebuses thundering, Spanish crossbows shooting bolts that could pierce completely through a man's body. Flint axes clashed against Spanish armor.

De Soto's horse went down, struck by eight arrows. The captain struggled free despite the weight of his armor, leaped upon another mount, and led a furious charge, scattering the Indians in all directions.

Some of the warriors waded into a broad pond, where they were surrounded. De Soto shouted that if they surrendered he would spare their lives. But they yelled back defiance, standing in water so deep that they had to lift one another to be able to aim their arrows. Many of them stayed in the water fighting for the next fourteen hours before struggling to shore to collapse. Others held out most of the following day and were pulled to the banks still resisting.

"Kill us now," they said. "We cannot bear the shame of losing."

But Hernando ordered his captives untied and fed, sending for the captured Chief Vitacucho, who insisted the whole battle had been a misunderstanding. De Soto accepted the feeble excuse politely and again offered his friendship. Nevertheless, he decided the prisoners would go with the Spaniards as hostages until they reached other lands.

Vitacucho continued to scheme. One day a valiant warrior, one who had been fiercest in defense of the pond, sat beside De Soto sharing a meal. Suddenly the man struck De Soto in the face with all his force while Vitacucho and other prisoners fought to escape. Vitacucho and De Soto's attacker were killed in the struggle, as were four Spaniards.

De Soto pressed northward to the Suwannee River, where they built a bridge to cross it. Then they moved on into the territory of the fearsome Apalachee nation, whose neighbors claimed were the fiercest warriors in the world. The Spaniards, endangered all the way by hidden archers, reached a large village on a site that later would become Tallahassee, Florida.

*The Suwannee River*

Since this was not far from the sea and the month was November, De Soto decided to spend the winter in this village and carefully explore the surrounding land, looking for good farmland or orchards. The ruler here was a famous chief, Capafi, who had fled but was probably not moving very rapidly. When De Soto finally captured him, Capafi turned out to be so monstrously fat that his legs would not support him and he had to go about on all fours. Even so, before long he somehow managed to escape.

One morning two young Indians appeared at the camp and told the soldiers of a region called Cofitachequi to the north. It had gold in abundance, they declared, much to the soldiers' excitement. De Soto, who had planned to go north in any case, waited only until winter was ending. Then, in March of 1540, he advanced into what is now the state of Georgia.

The hospitality of the Indians of Georgia delighted the Spaniards, as did the beauty of the land. A chief named Cofa proved so gracious in providing food and shelter that De Soto presented him with a remarkable gift: the single cannon they were transporting. This was not quite so generous as it seemed, since the cannon's weight and awkwardness was delaying the Spanish march.

Crossing streams and bridging rivers, they moved north, the hardest crossing being near the present city of Augusta, Georgia. The river was the Savannah.

North of the river they met six warriors clad in decorated deerskins. They were guarding a beautiful girl who seemed to be a princess, or at least a person of importance. She asked, through Ortiz the interpreter, if the Spaniards came in peace or for war. After De Soto spoke of friendship, she said he must

*The Savannah River near Augusta, Georgia*

*De Soto meeting Cofita*

wait until she spoke with the queen of her people. The girl and her guards left in bark canoes.

Several hours afterwards, the Savannah River was suddenly dotted with canoes. A large Indian party landed, carrying another girl, even more beautiful, on a litter. She was crowned with eagle feathers and dressed in soft white cotton. She spoke with dignity, explaining that crops were bad this year, but promising they would share what food they had with the Spaniards.

The queen, graceful and lovely, instantly won the admiration of the Spaniards, who called her Cofita, although that was probably not her real name. Her eyes were black but sparkling; in fact, they are described as much like Hernando De Soto's own eyes. She presented De Soto with a necklace of pearls.

The Spaniards were welcomed by Cofita's villagers, who were part of the large Creek tribe. The men were tall, athletic, and well dressed. No gold was to be found here, but when Cofita realized how eager the Spaniards were for pearls, she presented them with basketfuls.

Hernando might well have stayed to share this small kingdom with the beautiful Cofita, for this clearly was her wish. But he, of course, had other loyalties. Soon the Spaniards were on the march again, moving northward through lands now part of South and North Carolina. Later they even entered Tennessee.

In this region, the most highly civilized people they met were the Cherokees, who built towns surrounded by wooden stockades and created pottery that aroused the Spaniards' admiration. The Cherokees also pleased the Spanish soldiers with gifts of wild turkey and of fish caught in the Tennessee River. A scouting party Hernando sent out reported some mountains nearby, the Lookouts. Far more interesting was their report of a "huge cow with very big hooves and a humped back." For the first time, Europeans had seen an American bison.

Hernando decided it was time to turn southwest, expecting to reach the Gulf of Mexico and meet the ships he had sent to Cuba to deliver messages, then return. The friendly Cherokees lent him five hundred men as baggage carriers, and De Soto moved on.

Still well-treated by the Indians, the explorers moved farther into the present state of Alabama, following the important Coosa River. They soon reached the town of Talladega, a name still found as both a city and a county in Alabama.

Talladega was a pleasant place of cone-shaped bark huts and land forested with pines. It was so attractive, in fact, that the Spaniards spent two weeks there with the powerful Chief Cosa as their host. But when De Soto was ready to leave, the chief refused him the services of Indian carriers. They were nearing the end of Cherokee country, he explained. Besides, he wanted the Spaniards to remain and make a permanent settlement among his people.

*Chief Cosa of Talladega*

De Soto, who had studied the land carefully, was determined to complete his great circle of exploration and return to the sea before he made any decisions about settling. As always, he was cautious. Still, he told Cosa he would return later and left gifts of horses, hogs, and chickens, the first such birds in Alabama.

Before leaving, he was warned to be careful in the days ahead. Soon the Spaniards would reach the land of fierce Chief Tuscaloosa, whose Alibamus tribe awed their more peaceful neighbors.

Hernando knew that war lay ahead; this had been the story of his whole life. Yet nothing could have stopped him from striving to reach his goal. Regardless of risks, he would solve as many mysteries of North America as any man could.

But he would ask no soldier to risk more than he would. De Soto, with his black eyes and black pointed beard, took his place at the head of the column as they moved on to confront the much-feared Chief Tuscaloosa.

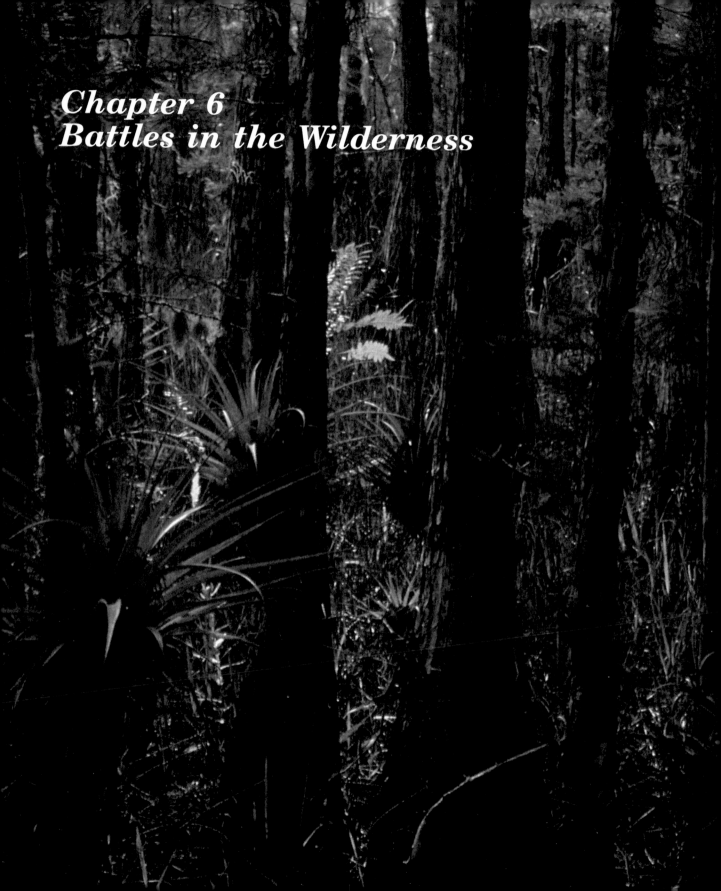

# Chapter 6
# Battles in the Wilderness

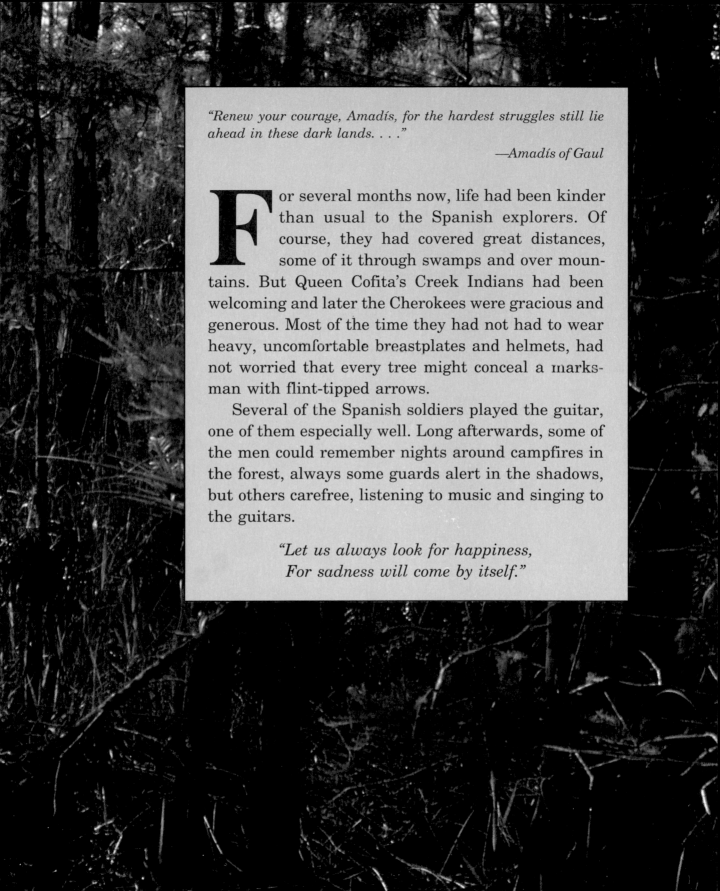

*"Renew your courage, Amadís, for the hardest struggles still lie ahead in these dark lands. . . ."*

—*Amadís of Gaul*

For several months now, life had been kinder than usual to the Spanish explorers. Of course, they had covered great distances, some of it through swamps and over mountains. But Queen Cofita's Creek Indians had been welcoming and later the Cherokees were gracious and generous. Most of the time they had not had to wear heavy, uncomfortable breastplates and helmets, had not worried that every tree might conceal a marksman with flint-tipped arrows.

Several of the Spanish soldiers played the guitar, one of them especially well. Long afterwards, some of the men could remember nights around campfires in the forest, always some guards alert in the shadows, but others carefree, listening to music and singing to the guitars.

*"Let us always look for happiness,*
*For sadness will come by itself."*

This was one of the popular songs of the time, one that De Soto himself had sung. The words were about to prove true: Sorrow was on the way.

Chief Tuscaloosa, whose lands they neared, led the most warlike tribe of a group of Indians known as the Muskhogean. They were allies, friends, and even distant cousins of the Creek Indians, but these people were little like Queen Cofita's peaceful villagers.

The Spaniards were moving along a well-marked trail—almost a road, as some of them called it later—when advance scouts reported that a company of armed Indians awaited them on a hill ahead.

De Soto moved ahead cautiously and soon approached these warriors. The Indians stood at attention, gazing into the distance, pretending that the Spaniards did not even exist. All of them were tall, but two seemed like giants to the Spaniards. One of them stood about six-and-a-half feet (two meters) tall and was dressed as a chief. The other towering warrior seemed to be his son.

All the Indians were splendidly dressed in beaded moccasins, headdresses of eagle plumes, and cloaks of brilliant colors. There could be no doubt which one was Chief Tuscaloosa, for he was seated in the center on a tree stump carved to resemble a throne. His feather cape was so long it brushed the ground.

De Soto, remembering how he had greeted Atahualpa long ago in Peru, led the cavalry forward in a dramatic show of horsemanship, but these Indians did not flinch. Instead, Tuscaloosa rose as De Soto dismounted and the two leaders moved toward each other. De Soto was known as a tall man among Spaniards, but Chief Tuscaloosa easily stood a head above him.

Through the interpreter, Tuscaloosa spoke words that would be remembered and written down later: "I greet you as a brother. In the next village lodgings have been prepared for you."

"Great Chief," De Soto replied, "I did not want to leave these lands without meeting you. I should be happy if we became friends, and I invite you to ride with me to the next village on one of our horses."

Tuscaloosa nodded, accepting, although he had never seen a horse before. The largest animal the Spaniards had was the only one able to carry this giant. When Tuscaloosa mounted, his moccasins nearly brushed the ground.

Soon they reached a village surrounded by a stockade of sharpened logs. Tuscaloosa gestured, showing De Soto a house where he could stay. The chief, after dismounting, walked with dignity to another house, his own.

*Indian village surrounded by a protective stockade of logs*

In spite of Tuscaloosa's stony-faced assurances of friendship, De Soto felt uneasy. Soon two Spaniards disappeared, and De Soto strongly suspected they had been murdered in the forest. A clash of wills came when De Soto requested help to carry supplies to the next town, a place supposed to be the largest settlement in Tuscaloosa's domain. When the giant insolently refused, De Soto called on him with several armored soldiers and invited Tuscaloosa to join them on the march. This invitation seemed very much like a threat, and Tuscaloosa agreed to join the Spaniards on the journey to Mauvila, a place we now call Mobile in Alabama.

De Soto presented Tuscaloosa with a pair of boots so huge that no Spaniard could wear them and a handsome but very long red velvet cloak. The chief donned them proudly but silently.

As they began their journey, De Soto tried to explain to the chief that the name of the town, Mauvila, reminded him of his favorite story, for in one of the adventures of Amadís is a princess named Mabilia. No one knows what Tuscaloosa thought of this strange tale of knighthood.

But while Hernando chatted pleasantly of Amadís, he was taking precautions. Scouts who had hurried ahead returned to warn him that the town ahead swarmed with warriors, many hiding in large log houses. Military drills had been started so the different tribes gathered to destroy De Soto would know each other's ways of attack.

Hernando approached what is now Mobile, Alabama, on a morning in October 1540. He saw a large town fortified by a high stockade that enclosed scores of log buildings. Some were family houses, while oth-crs were large enough to hold hundreds of warriors. De Soto paused with his advance guard, deciding that the bulk of his army, which would arrive later, would camp on a plain outside town. It seemed safer to be outside the stockade.

With two hundred men, De Soto made a proud and defiant entrance into Mobile. He accepted a house Tuscaloosa had arranged for him, but warned his officers not to lay down their weapons for a moment. He calmly watched an entertainment of song and dance arranged in his honor, and he praised the grace and beauty of the local women.

He knew the Indians were waiting for some signal to attack, but the battle exploded instead by accident when a hotheaded warrior assaulted interpreter Juan Ortiz.

Suddenly havoc spread through the streets with yells, shouts, and curses. De Soto gathered together the third of his army that had already arrived on the plain outside town.

Not all the Spaniards were lucky enough to get outside the stockade when the fighting erupted. Thirteen men—eight soldiers, two missionary priests, two black servants, and an Indian friend from another region—were besieged inside a log house near the center of the town. The priests were unarmed, the soldiers carried halberds and three crossbows, and the Indian had a bow and arrows. They barricaded the entrance, hoping and praying to hold out until rescued.

Meanwhile, De Soto hurled a cavalry charge across the plain, horses galloping, lances pointed, riders yelling the Spanish battle cry of "Santiago!" as trumpets blared.

*The bloody battle of Mobile*

The Indians stood their ground, leaping into the air to seize the Spanish lances, hoping to drag the riders from their saddles. In a few cases they succeeded. But the stronger weapons of the Spaniards soon drove the Indians behind the shelter of the stockade. From there they shot arrows and waved in the air the bloody scalps of Spaniards already slain.

De Soto was furious, enraged not only by Tuscaloosa's treachery, but also because the Indians had seized most of the Spaniards' supplies and the two hundred pounds (ninety kilograms) of pearls from Queen Cofita. At the same time, he was alarmed about his thirteen companions trapped inside the town. Tuscaloosa, he vowed, would pay for this.

He charged the wooden wall with both cavalry and infantry, he himself spearheading the column as usual. The first hour was a time of savage bloodletting on both sides, for it seemed that neither the ten thousand Indian warriors nor the small army of Spaniards could triumph.

De Soto charged again and again, then shifted his plan of battle. His best horsemen dismounted and, carrying axes, rushed to chop the ropes holding the logs of the stockade and its gate together. Their shields protected them from a fierce rain of arrows, while booming harquebuses drove the Indians from the top of the fence.

At the same time, the danger to the thirteen men trapped in the log house became grave. Indians, unable to chop through the logs, were cutting holes in the thatched roof and plunging inside. There they fought hand to hand with the besieged soldiers and priests, who could surely not hold out long.

A battle to the death raged through Mobile, house to house, no one fleeing or yielding. Many Indians, sensing defeat, set fire to their own houses, choosing to burn themselves alive inside rather than surrender. Women seized the weapons of fallen warriors and fought valiantly.

De Soto hacked his way to the center of the town, his finest soldiers beside him. Eventually he was able to rescue the besieged men in the house, who had now survived more than an hour of relentless attack by enemies leaping through the roof. Not one of the defenders had been killed, but the scene of death in the log house was horrible.

Later, after victory, De Soto said this was the hardest, fiercest, most costly battle he had fought against Indians anywhere. Other veterans of wars in Panama and Peru agreed with him. The battle of Mobile, fought against the Alibamus Indians, was among the most terrible in the long history of Spanish conquest.

Tuscaloosa himself had disappeared, but most of the Spanish supplies had been burned or stolen, and the precious load of pearls was never found. De Soto had suffered a painful wound in the thigh, yet had forced himself to stay in the saddle and fight for two more hours, despite being weakened by loss of blood. Thirty Spaniards lay dead, and they had lost forty horses. At least 250 Spanish soldiers suffered serious wounds.

Night fell on the battlefield as the Spaniards made their camp among thousands of Indian dead. De Soto, summoning all his strength, made new plans. Since landing in Florida, he had lost more than a hundred men, and at this moment there was probably not a man in the camp without at least a minor wound. He would let his battered army recover here in Mobile; he would rebuild the stockade.

During the next days De Soto learned from a messenger that he was camped only five days' journey from the sea, where ships from Cuba were searching for him to exchange news and deliver supplies. All this seemed perfect for his plans of establishing a permanent Spanish colony. The town would be here, at Mobile, on a broad river that swept into a huge bay.

However, De Soto had lost none of the caution that had served him well all his life. At night he would stroll quietly through the camp, overhearing conversations, learning how the soldiers felt. Many, he discovered, were on the point of desertion. If he moved nearer the sea, if boats were sighted, this would be the end of his army.

So, without letting anyone know his secret thoughts, he broke camp on November 18, 1540, and moved northward, away from the Gulf of Mexico.

They struggled across rivers that were broad and swift, the Black Warrior and the Tombigbee. Soon the Spaniards reached the lands of an advanced and civilized Indian people, the Chicasaw. A village of about two hundred houses had been deserted by its inhabitants but, luckily, food had been left behind.

Finally the Chicasaw chief was persuaded to pay a visit to the Spaniards. He arrived with a most welcome gift: hundreds of rabbits and bundles of pelts and capes. The clothing was especially needed by those soldiers who had lost most of their clothes in the struggle at Mobile.

Spring came, it was time for the Spaniards to move on, but De Soto sensed that the Chicasaw, despite their acts of friendship, were plotting. Hernando ordered the men to sleep with their arms beside them, to be constantly on guard.

The Chicasaw swooped upon the village long before dawn, yelling, beating drums, and ringing bells. Flaming arrows set fire to huts where the Spaniards had slept. There followed a scene of wild confusion— the din of battle, the squeals of pigs, and whinnying of horses. Two hours later, as the sun arose, the Spaniards had already carried the day. Though not wounded, De Soto suffered bruises when he fell from his horse because an aide had not properly cinched the saddle.

*Warrior of the American Southeast*

The fight claimed the lives of a dozen soldiers and the courageous Francisca Hinestrosa, the only woman in the expedition. She had given outstanding service in serving food and caring for the sick and wounded. Fifty horses had been lost, some killed or stolen, others simply stampeded. These would add to the herds of wild horses in North America.

The Spaniards pushed on. At a neighboring village they let the wounded rest, while blacksmiths set up a forge using a bellows they made of bearskin. They had to repair arms, saddles, and tools. Then the column took up the march again.

De Soto moved north because a scout had reported a strange building and settlement called the Fort of Alibamo. It was constructed of several stockades, one within the other, and a stream flowed in front of its gates, protecting them as a moat guards a castle.

Here were a different kind of Indian, men who wore headdresses decorated with both feathers and horns. These were the Muskhogee, famed for their bravery, recognizable by the black and red paint they wore on their faces as signs of ferocity.

De Soto decided to attack and capture this fortified town of Alibamo. Dividing his army into three columns, he charged the fort's three barricaded entrances at the same time.

Such action was unlike Hernando's usual conduct. His nature was to send messengers of peace, to offer friendship and only use force when other means failed. Probably both De Soto and his men were angry and desperate after their troubles with Chief Tuscaloosa. Also, they must have needed food and other supplies with no delay, so they attacked the outer wall of this center.

*Declaration of war by Indians of southern North America*

Warriors appeared at the top of the stockade, shooting arrows and brandishing spears. But a gate gave way and soon the battle was raging inside the town itself. The Indians, realizing they could not overcome Spanish weapons, retreated, leaving De Soto in possession of the town. He ordered his men to defend the stockade.

Meanwhile, the Indians were gathering on the other side of a nearby river, the Tallahatchie. A frail bridge built by the Muskhogee spanned this stream. Hernando completely surprised the Indians by launching a charge from the stockade, crossing the bridge, and attacking.

The Spaniards were victorious but lost eight men killed in battle while twenty-five were wounded. They stayed at the fort four days to rest and recover, then pressed ahead, crossing rugged country to a village called Quizquiz.

The aged chief of Quizquiz was friendly, offered food, and spoke of a magnificent river just to the north. This was the first time any European had heard the name Mississippi.

Other Spanish explorers of the time probably would have turned back long before when they saw no sign of gold or silver. But Hernando De Soto was as drawn by the lure of the great river as others were impelled by the hope of treasure. Perhaps Hernando also had another thought in mind: If the great river flowed south to the Gulf of Mexico, his battered army might build boats and so find a way back to Cuba. Hernando,

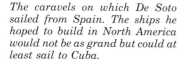

*The caravels on which De Soto sailed from Spain. The ships he hoped to build in North America would not be as grand but could at least sail to Cuba.*

who was both curious and practical, no doubt considered both things.

Weary and not really recovered from the wound he received at Mobile, Hernando ordered the men to gather all the food they could find, then to move on. No matter what the distance and danger, he would see this colossal stream with his own eyes.

Four days later, after struggling through swamps, they reached higher ground. Historians have argued for years about the exact spot they reached. It seems likely that place is now known as Commerce Landing in northwestern Mississippi, a few miles south of the Tennessee border.

Hernando, catching sight of the water, ordered the column to halt. Before him rolled the great river, even more marvelous than he had been told, great beyond any Spaniard's imagining of it.

*De Soto at the Mississippi*

# Chapter 7
# Beyond the River

*"Rolling, rolling from Arkansas, Kansas, Iowa,*
*Rolling from Ohio, Wisconsin, Illinois,*
*Rolling and shouting:*
*Till at last it is Mississippi,*
*The Father of Waters."*

—Stephen Vincent Benet

Most men, after reaching this huge barrier of water after so much struggle, might have stopped, turned back, or at least taken a long rest. But Hernando De Soto seemed eager only to cross the two miles (three kilometers) of water that lay before him, to know what lay beyond.

Pushing through pine thickets, he found a clear and level spot to set up a forge and then ordered work to begin at once on rafts or barges for the crossing. The sight of the magnificent river lifted the men's spirits. Long afterward some of them remembered how renewed they felt, how much fresher.

They had reasons for being worn out. By a route that often twisted and turned back upon itself, they had journeyed through what is now Florida, Georgia, South Carolina, and corners of North Carolina and Tennessee. They had zigzagged through Alabama in a great loop, then walked more than the width of Mississippi. Often they had fought their way almost step by step.

Even so, they were not building rafts to travel down the river toward the sea, but to go across it.

The Spaniards had finished four large rafts rigged with crude sails and oars when a long line of big canoes, rowed by about two hundred Indians, appeared on the river. A regal chief, without coming ashore, had himself announced as the ruler of Aquixo, as these lands were called.

By arriving with so many men and boats, he clearly meant to show his power; this was a warning. Yet he brought a gift of fish and bundles of cakes made from crushed prunes, which the Spaniards found had a good, faintly sweet taste.

De Soto thanked the chief for the supplies and asked him to come ashore so they might become better acquainted. Hernando invited the chief to become a friend.

The Indian stared at De Soto in silence and distrust, but then left without saying a word. The Spaniards marveled at how skillfully these Indians handled their canoes. Clearly the river was home to them.

De Soto spent almost three weeks building the barges. The harquebuses had become useless after the battle at Mobile since there was no more gunpowder, so the iron was melted down to make nails and other fasteners for the rafts.

*A Georgia chieftain*

The Spaniards, not without fear, actually crossed the Mississippi on June 18, 1541. They were afraid of strange currents, of concealed whirlpools, of attack by Indians in fast canoes. Very likely they would be assailed by the Indians when they landed, but they could not be sure since it was difficult to see a man on the opposite bank of a river so wide.

In spite of their fears the landing was made safely, but there was little time to rest or celebrate the crossing. De Soto at once ordered the rafts to be taken apart and every single nail and fastener carefully preserved. He was planning for the future and saw that other boats might be needed.

*Indians of Aquixo greeting De Soto in a fleet of canoes*

The Spaniards had landed in what is now the state of Arkansas. They described the country as rough and rugged with few inhabitants. De Soto kept his column close to the riverbank, following a path that led north for five days. Then he saw ahead a village of considerable size, and Indians told him he was in a region called Casqui. The Casqui chief sent messengers to give friendly greetings and a welcome to De Soto's men.

The Indians of Casqui seemed fascinated by these strange, pale visitors. They built them special shelters of branches and put on entertainments of song and dance to the beat of drums and the blowing of whistles. The Spaniards enjoyed the hospitality of these people for six days and later recalled the beauty of the Casqui women who danced.

*De Soto encounters Indians of the Mississippi River Valley*

The chief approached De Soto and spoke to him with great seriousness. A Spanish soldier who heard his words wrote them down long afterwards: "We know you are the Children of the Sun. Your weapons are more powerful than ours, and so must your religion be. Our newly sown fields are in need of water. Ask your God for rain and we will worship him."

De Soto, showing that he had not only faith but courage, assured the chief that bringing rain was not difficult. He ordered a great cross of pine to be built atop a hill, and three days later it was blessed in rites performed by the Spanish priests. Word must have spread through the surrounding country that something marvelous was taking place, for thousands of Indians arrived to see the strange ceremonies and, the Spaniards hoped, witness a miracle.

*Falls of the Ouachita River, which the De Soto expedition may have crossed in Arkansas*

The next day clouds rolled in, darkening the sky. Soon rain poured upon the parched fields while both Spaniards and Indians rejoiced.

The Spaniards moved on, deeper into the rugged land of Arkansas. De Soto met Indians who were wandering traders, and they told him of a range of mountains to the north where precious metals could be found. Hernando seems not to have had much faith in their report, for he sent only two soldiers on a prospecting mission, while he himself continued on.

When he reached the edge of the plains, he found only a few small villages, but there were herds of buffalo to provide the Spaniards with food and with robes for warmth.

News about the northern mountains seems to have been what De Soto already expected: the two soldiers came back from the edge of the Ozarks with neither gold nor silver. The best they found were some pieces of rock salt.

The army turned southwest. Perhaps De Soto had a faint hope of finding the fabled Seven Cities of Cibola that had so excited Cabeza de Vaca, although he admitted never having seen them. Actually, these golden towns were as imaginary as the tales of Amadís, but many men would lose their lives trying to find them in the North American desert. De Soto may have believed some of the tales of the cities of Cibola, but there is no sign he thought they were nearby. Perhaps he mentioned them to his men to give them hope and keep them pressing ahead.

He moved his column west along the banks of the powerful Arkansas River, entering a land known as Tula. The Tula Indians were not frightened by the sight of gleaming armor or such strange animals as horses. Instead of fleeing when the Spaniards entered their village, they flew to arms. The battle lasted until darkness forced a halt in the fighting, and in the morning the Indians were found to have retreated. De Soto's men moved into the empty village, needing time for the wounded to heal.

Three nights later the Tula Indians burst out of the concealing darkness and another terrible fight took place, but again Spanish weapons proved better. The Indians retreated into the dawn, carrying or dragging their wounded. Peace was made a day later, the Tulas bringing gifts of dried meat and other food.

Winter was coming, making it important to find a place to make camp. Country to the southeast, a province called Autiamque, might be the right choice since corn was supposed to be plentiful there. When they reached its main settlement, they found the houses were good and the food abundant.

De Soto's hopes were high as they prepared to spend the three winter months. In the spring, he told his officers, they would return to the Great River. There they could build boats, sail downstream, and somehow reach Cuba. In Cuba they could find new, vigorous men to join them in returning here. They would explore all the land to the west and establish Spanish settlements. Indeed, many of the common soldiers were looking at the rich land with longing, thinking that they would never be able to own such farms in Spain.

It was a glorious dream, and even the bitter winds and snows of Arkansas that winter did not dim their hope. So, huddled in the bark and log houses of their camp, they looked forward to spring, not knowing that their worst hardships still lay ahead.

Chapter 8
The Final Struggle

The Spaniards were so eager to return to the Great River that they hardly waited for spring to break camp. They had not spent the three winter months in idleness. As a good commander, De Soto knew his men had to be kept busy or they might turn quarrelsome and bored. He held drills and ordered hunting parties to find rabbits for the stew pots. On March 6, 1542, as soon as the snow thawed, they were on their way.

Soon they became aware that one of their company had disappeared. His name was Don Diego de Guzmán, and he came from Seville. Handsome, witty, and an eager gambler, Guzmán was among the most popular younger men of the expedition. De Soto, alarmed by Guzmán's absence, stopped the march and sent out search parties.

A few days later, it was learned that nothing terrible had happened to the young squire. In fact, it was just the opposite. The chieftain of a nearby tribe had taken a liking to Guzmán, invited him to stay in his village, and given him his beautiful daughter in marriage.

A written message was sent to the young man asking him to return. The reply came written by Guzmán on deerskin: They were not to worry about him but to leave him alone. He had everything he wanted right where he was.

De Soto saw no point in trying to find the young man and force him back with the expedition. So Don Diego de Guzmán, in this unusual way, became the first European settler in what is now the United States.

The Spanish army now numbered about thirteen hundred men, including perhaps six hundred Indians who had joined them at different places. They would need such a force and even more as they entered the lands of the hostile chief of Anilco. This proud and fierce ruler did not attack the column openly, but his warriors shot arrows from hiding and set upon any small group foolish enough to lag behind or stray. Juan Ortiz, the Spaniards' interpreter, had died during the winter at Autiamque, so negotiating friendship with the Indians was now very difficult.

They marched southeast, hoping to reach the Mississippi River once again. On the way, they trudged through tangled, watery swamps where alligators lurked and insects hovered in swarms sometimes so dense that they resembled clouds of mist or steam. Every step was perilous and difficult.

Now near the end of their expedition, they hoped, the days seemed much like the hard times in Florida

*De Soto's men trudged through alligator-infested swamps.*

when they had fought their way across marshes, knee-deep or even waist-deep in murky water. Their armor and helmets, in spite of winter polishing, showed signs of rust. Many complained about how bad their spears had become, with their iron or steel heads lost and replaced with flint.

At last they knew by changes in the land and vegetation that they were nearing the Mississippi. This thought, the memory of the mighty stream, cheered Hernando. He told his companions he felt as if he were going to meet an old friend, the river. At last, breaking free of the snarled vines of the swamp, he saw the rolling waters again.

De Soto camped on the western bank of the Mississippi, in what is believed to be southeastern Arkansas, on April 17, 1542. The Indians, after some initial threats, turned friendly, bringing food. Here, Hernando thought, he might build boats to reach Cuba.

The chief of Guachoya, a Quapaw settlement, paid a solemn visit to De Soto. His people lived in villages protected by log stockades. Each house was raised on a mound of earth so floors would be dry during heavy rains. The people were both farmers and fishermen.

To the Spaniards, the appearance of the Quapaws was very strange. They painted their bodies in half a dozen colors, they wore bobcat furs adorned by little clumps of feathers, and other pelts decorated their ankles. The men carried bells fashioned from gourds, and as they walked or gestured, seashells strung into bracelets and necklaces clicked together.

After a long ceremony of smoking a peace pipe, De Soto explained the main beliefs of the Christian religion, but the chief showed little interest. The Mississippi River and the sun, he replied, were all-powerful to him and his people. Yet he felt there must be a connection between De Soto and the river gods. De Soto, because of all he had done, had to be immortal, especially linked to the spirit world. The chief bowed and left after promising to send supplies daily.

The Spaniards had reached a point where they were surrounded by swamps, dense thickets of reeds, and forests almost impossible to cross. Worse, the mosquitoes here carried the dread disease of malaria, although the Spaniards did not suspect it was the sting of these insects that caused the terrible fever. They blamed the water, the air, the food, almost anything except the real source of the illness.

Soon Hernando began to show signs of this disease, burning with fever, then shivering as chills seized him even on the hottest days. In the past he had seemed to conquer illnesses and wounds by sheer will power, pretending he felt no pain or weakness. He was a man of such strength and health that he could recover soon from almost any sickness or injury. But now it was different. He was forced to rest, lying on a bed his men made for him.

Still, his curiosity, his hunger to learn more, would not let him stay quiet. He had heard of the Natchez Indians on the eastern side of the river and knew they wove fine cloth and made exquisite pottery. They worshipped the sun, he was told, and had the odd custom of flattening the heads of boys from babyhood by tying bark or thin planks tightly about their skulls. De Soto could not resist trying to see this for himself. Such impulses to see more, know more, were the story of his life.

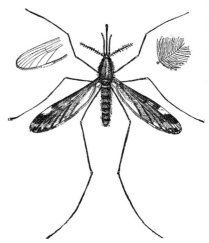

*The Anopheles mosquito, whose bite transmits organisms that cause malaria*

Summoning his failing strength, he crossed the river again, but was disappointed to find only deserted villages and to hear threatening messages from the chief of the Natchez people. He returned to the western bank.

Although the Indians of Guachoya remained friendly, other Indians of the region lurked as a constant threat. De Soto felt their position was dangerous when, about May 14, his fever rose so sharply that he could no longer stand or walk. During the next three days he was racked by fever and chills, yet remained in command, ordering guards to be carefully posted, lookouts always alert. He did not trust the Indians around them, friendly though they seemed at the moment.

Facing death, he brought out a long, detailed will and had it read aloud before witnesses. In it he provided for Isabel, his family, and several friends. As the will was being read, tears ran down the cheeks of his officers. De Soto thanked them for their loyalty and asked them to leave him alone with a priest for a short time so he might make a final confession. Then they were to return so a new leader could be chosen. Even with death almost upon him, he carried out his duties to the men he commanded.

When they came back, De Soto said he thought it was best that they should elect their own commander, but all the officers felt this must be De Soto's decision. Hernando named Captain Luis Moscoso, who had shared adventures with him first in Peru. The officers swore allegiance to Moscoso.

Hernando De Soto fought his last battle, the struggle against malaria, for another five days, losing his fight for life on May 21, 1542. This was just a little over a year after his first sighting of the Mississippi.

Many of the soldiers felt they had lost a father, and all knew they had lost a great leader. They also felt a new danger. The Indians had hailed De Soto as immortal. Would his death destroy their belief in Spanish power? It seemed likely and perhaps fatal.

Hernando's death was kept secret. The guards were changed with unusual frequency, while exercises were held to show that an active commander was still in charge. Everything was done to try to make it seem that De Soto was alive and healthy. But secretly De Soto was buried in the dark of the night.

Everyone felt uneasy about the burial. What if the Indians discovered the grave? The captains met, and one of them, Nuño de Tovar, spoke for all of them:

*Burial of De Soto in the waters of the Mississippi*

"Since his memory and his glory are forever bound to this great, ever moving river, let us entrust it with the task of keeping safely, for all eternity, the body of our beloved general. I propose that we find the deepest place and that we lay his body to rest there, at night, without the knowledge of the Indians."

The captains, in small boats, went out on the river pretending to fish, but actually testing for depth. Halfway across, they found the deepest spot.

That night they cut down a tree trunk of heavy oak wood, then carved it into a coffin. De Soto's body was reverently placed in this and carried out onto the river on their largest boat. A dozen silent men, some of them weeping, carried De Soto on this final journey. They let the strange coffin of American green oak slide gently into the waters. Hernando De Soto and the Father of Waters were now one forever.

W hen the chief of Guachoya came to the Spanish camp and asked to see De Soto, the new leader, Moscoso, said that Hernando had gone to visit his father, the Sun. The chief accepted this, but the Spaniards realized that to stay longer was dangerous. They felt there was no time to build boats that could survive the currents of the Mississippi, then the waves of the Gulf of Mexico. Hernando's plan to sail to Havana and bring back new settlers seemed beyond their strength.

They broke camp quickly after deciding that they could not be far from the Spanish colony in New Spain, as Mexico was then called. They would march west and then south. After all, they agreed in a council meeting, they were not sailors and there was not a pilot among them.

So the column was again on the move, but this time without the leadership of De Soto. After many struggles and hardships, they crossed Arkansas again and entered the present state of Texas.

The plains of Texas seemed endless, the people few and scattered. Since both men and horses were worn out from day after day of walking, they moved much more slowly than before. They also lacked the spirit that De Soto had given them. Somewhere in the region of the Neches and Trinity rivers, they decided to turn back and try to follow the plan Hernando had first given them.

*De Soto's remaining men fight their way down the Mississippi.*

So, in a sense, De Soto was still in command, even after death. If they had followed his advice at once, they would have spared a year of wasted suffering.

Back on the banks of the Mississippi, they managed to build seven boats with awkward sails made of leather and what was left of their cloaks. Those who survived, only 311 men, set sail on the river, pursued by Indians in canoes. They defended themselves with crossbows, since there was no gunpowder.

After making an amazing voyage of seventeen days during hurricane season along the Gulf coast, they reached a Spanish settlement that is now the seaport of Tampico, Mexico. Their great adventure had ended in the year 1543, probably in the month of September.

Not only had they made a gruelling sea voyage in the most makeshift boats, but they had walked across land that is now in nine states: Florida, Georgia, South Carolina, North Carolina, Tennessee, Alabama, Mississippi, Arkansas, and Texas.

Hernando De Soto did not live to see any part of his dream come true. He never realized his hope of settling the vast territory he had explored. He had found no gold, but he had seen things that in time would prove far more valuable: great farmlands and forests, rivers that would one day be routes of trade. In traveling more than 2,000 miles (3,219 kilometers) through the wilderness, he had added immeasurably to the old world's knowledge of the new.

*De Soto and his men were the first Europeans to see such spots as the beautiful Savannah River in present-day Georgia.*

Hernando stands out in history as a true explorer, not just a treasure hunter. De Soto was human enough to look for riches, but like his hero, Amadís of Gaul, he always longed to see the hill that lay beyond the next hill, and then the next.

In an age remembered for the cruelty of its leaders, De Soto was one of the rare commanders who did not inflict mass torture, who did not destroy whole tribes of Indians simply for the sake of killing or in a vague hope of booty. He tried to be a man of honor and, as one who kept his word, he towers above the other great explorers and conquerors of his time.

A great historian of Peru, Ricardo Palma, after studying the conquest of the Incas wrote, "Hernando

*Portrait of Hernando De Soto*

De Soto was truly chivalrous and he may have been the only noble mind among the 170 Spaniards who took the Child of the Sun prisoner."

De Soto lived in a time and a world where looting and cruelty were not only accepted but often praised. He shared many of the faults of his times and did not always live up to the knightly ideals he admired. Yet he was far more than a mere treasure hunter or a warrior seeking slaves. Hernando De Soto, leading his men through the wilderness to the banks of the great river, showed the character of the true explorer: a determination to see what lies beyond the next hill and then the one after that, no matter how far away those hills lie or how hard the journey.

*De Soto's expedition venturing upon the unknown Florida coast*

# Appendices

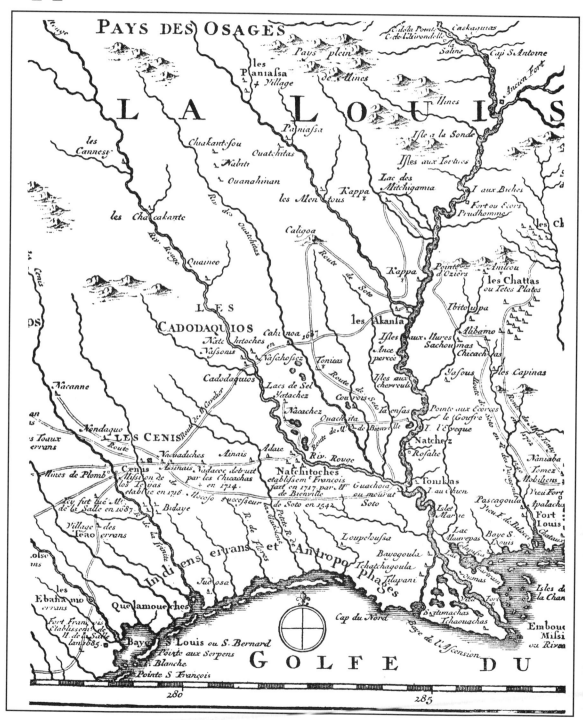

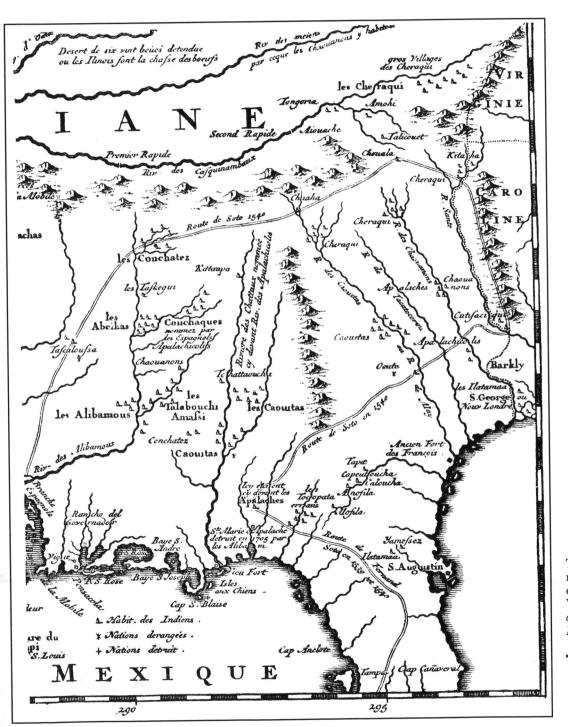

This map of De Soto's route appeared in a 1707 edition of Garcilaso de la Vega's *Story of the Incas and of the Conquest of la Florida.*

Title page of Gonzalo Fernandez de Oviedo's history of the West Indies. Oviedo sailed with Pedrarias to the New World in 1514, as did De Soto. Charles V of Spain later appointed Oviedo as the official historian for the New World.

Title page of a history of the Americas by Spanish historian Antonio de Herrera y Tordesillas. Herrera's work covers explorations made from 1492 to 1554. The volume shown here is decorated with portraits of famous Inca chiefs.

# Timeline of Events in De Soto's Lifetime

**About 1500**—Hernando De Soto is born Jerez de los Caballeros in Spain's Extremadura region; Pedro Cabral reaches the coast of Brazil and claims it for Portugal

**1502**—Christopher Columbus, on his fourth voyage, explores the coast of Panama

**1513**—Vasco Núñez de Balboa discovers the Pacific Ocean

**1514**—De Soto embarks on his first voyage to the New World, sailing with Pedrarias, new governor of Darién (Panama)

**1519**—Pedrarias executes Balboa; Ferdinand Magellan begins his voyage to circumnavigate the globe

**1521**—Hernando Cortés conquers Mexico's Aztec Indians

**1525**—De Soto takes part in the conquest of Nicaragua and settles there as a mine operator

**1531-1535**—Under Francisco Pizarro, De Soto is a leader in the conquest of the Incas

**1533**—Pizarro executes Atahualpa, king of the Incas; Pizarro and De Soto march to Cuzco

**1534**—De Soto becomes Spanish governor of Cuzco

**1535-1536** —De Soto leaves Peru, sails back to Spain, and marries Pedrarias's daughter Isabel

**1537**—King Charles appoints De Soto governor of Cuba and royal deputy of the Floridas

**1538**—De Soto's fleet leaves Spain for Florida

**1539**—De Soto's expedition lands off the coast of Florida near Tampa Bay on May 25

**1539-1542** —De Soto and his men travel through present-day Florida, Georgia, South Carolina, North Carolina, Tennessee, Alabama, Mississippi, and Arkansas

**1540**—De Soto vanquishes Indians at Mauvila (Battle of Mobile)

**1541** —De Soto reaches the Mississippi River on May 8 and crosses it on June 18

**1542**—Hernando De Soto dies in the province of Guachoya on the west bank of the Mississippi River on May 21; recent research suggests that the location of his death, formerly believed to be in Louisiana, is in southeast Arkansas; under Luis de Moscoso, De Soto's men travel to Texas, back to the Mississippi, and on into the Gulf of Mexico, landing at Tampico, Mexico, in 1543

# Glossary of Terms

**avalanche**—A falling mass of earth, rocks, or snow down a mountainside

**besieged**—Surrounded by an enemy force

**booty**—Goods taken by the victor in war

**brandish**—To hold out a weapon in a threatening way

**breadth**—Distance from side to side; width

**chasm**—A deep space or opening in the earth's surface

**chivalry**—The gallant, courteous behavior of an ideal knight

**equator**—An imaginary east-west line around the earth, halfway between the north and south poles

**ferocity**—A fierce or violent manner

**flagship**—The ship that carries the commander of a fleet and flies his flag

**flinch**—To shrink back in fear or pain

**gangplank**—A bridge set up between a ship and the pier for boarding and loading cargo

**halberd**—A battle-ax with a spearhead on the end

**harquebus**—A heavy but portable gun, usually fired from a support

**hemisphere**—One-half of the earth's surface; the earth is usually divided into its northern and southern hemispheres or its eastern and western hemispheres

**isthmus**—A narrow strip of land between two bodies of water

**litter**—A bed or seat on which a sick person can be carried

**llama**—A South American animal related to the camel

**loincloth**—A piece of clothing consisting of a cloth hanging from the hips

**makeshift**—A crudely made item for temporary use

**malaria**—A disease producing chills and fever and caused by parasites transmitted by a mosquito

**mangrove**—Trees with large roots above the surface that grow in or near water

**Mass**—A Catholic ceremony that recalls Jesus' Last Supper

**page**—A boy serving at a royal court or training to be a knight

**ransom**—Money paid to release a prisoner or hostage

**rout**—To disorganize, defeat, or put to flight

**Santiago**—In English, St. James; the patron saint of Spain

**stature**—Height or importance

**stockade**—An enclosure made of posts to protect or imprison

**treachery**—Disloyalty, faithlessness, or betrayal

**vanguard**—People moving forward at the head of a march or procession

# Bibliography

## For further reading, see:

Hemming, John. *The Conquest of the Incas*. NY: Harcourt, Brace Jovanovich, 1970.

Maynard, Theodore. *De Soto and the Conquistadores*. Reprint of 1930 edition. NY: AMS Press, 1978.

Montgomery, Elizabeth Rider. *A World Explorer: Hernando De Soto*. Champaign, IL: Garrard Pub. Co., 1964.

Swanton, John R. *Final Report of the United States De Soto Expedition Commission*. Reprint of 1939 edition. Washington, D.C.: Smithsonian Institution Press, 1985. (For older readers.)

Syme, Ronald. *De Soto: Finder of the Mississippi*. NY: Morrow, 1957.

Garcilaso de la Vega. *The Florida of the Inca*. Translated and edited by John G. Varner and Jeanette J. Varner. Austin: The University of Texas Press, 1951. (For older readers.)

# Index

**Page numbers in boldface type indicate illustrations.**

## Picture Identifications for Chapter Opening Spreads

6-7— View along the Mississippi River

10-11—Town in the Extremadura region of Spain

24-25—Map of the isthmus of Panama

40-41—Tiahuanacu, a pre-Inca city in the Andes

62-63—Egrets and wood storks

80-81—Florida cypresses

94-95—Mist rising from the Mississippi River at sunrise

102-103—Cypress grove in Tennessee

110-111—Dawn in the wilds of Florida

## Acknowledgment

For a critical reading of the manuscript, our thanks to John Parker, Ph.D., Curator, James Ford Bell Library, University of Minnesota, Minneapolis, Minnesota

## Picture Acknowledgments

Arkansas History Commission—9, 67

The Bettmann Archive—58, 70, 75, 86, 92, 93, 98

© Jerry Hennen—6-7, 30

Historical Pictures Service, Chicago—18, 27, 28, 29, 33, 34, 39

North Wind Picture Archives—2, 4, 13, 15, 17, 19, 21, 23, 24-25, 31, 32, 36, 38, 40-41, 42, 45, 46 (2 pictures), 47, 49, 51, 53, 56, 57 (2 pictures), 60, 61 (2 pictures), 71, 73, 79, 83, 89, 91, 96, 97, 99, 105, 107, 109, 112, 113, 114, 115, 116-117, 118, 119

Odyssey Productions: © Robert Frerck—10-11, 16, 59

Chip and Rosa Maria de la Cueva Peterson—37

Tom Stack & Associates: © Larry Lipsky—65; © M. Timothy O'Keefe—72 (margin)

© Lynn M. Stone—62-63, 80-81

SuperStock International—5

Tony Stone Worldwide/Chicago, Ltd.: © Charles McNulty—76; © Lynn M. Stone—110-111; © Tom Till—94-95

Valan Photos: © Stephen J. Krasemann—75; © Robert C. Simpson—72 (top); © Wouterloot-Gregoire—102-103

## About the Author

Robert Carson was born in Michigan and received a Bachelor of Arts degree from Michigan State University at Ann Arbor. He did advanced study at the School of the National Museum of Anthropology in Mexico, where he now lives. Mr. Carson has written ten novels, and his work has appeared in *The Atlantic*, *American Heritage*, and other magazines. His interest in Hernando de Soto was increased when he wrote the Mississippi volume for Childrens Press's America the Beautiful series.